Learning to
Live From
the Heart

My Stories & Lessons

Stephan van Coppenole

First paperback edition December 2024
First ebook edition December 2024

Cover design by Don Huff

ISBN 979-8-9916080-0-8 (paperback)
ISBN 979-8-9916080-1-5 (ebook)

Published by Bearded Man Publishing
www.beardedmanpublishing.com

iii

This book is dedicated to my mother, Marline.
She has shown me unconditional love throughout my life,
even if I couldn't see it
until my early 30's.

Table of Contents

Prologue

Preface 1

1. Deciding to Align With Love..5

    The Story of the Green Wig

Facing Fears 17

2. What I Fear, I Must Do...19

    The Story of Free Hugs

3. Making a Game Out of It 29

    The Story of the Hugging Contest

4. Staying Connected Despite the Fear....................................36

    The Story of Public Speaking

5. Diffusing the Fear 46

    The Story of Rollercoasters

6. Planning for the Best, Prepared for the Worst.....................54

    The Story of Unemployment

Building Habits 75

7. Building Willpower 77

    The Story of the Promise Book

8. Changing Habits 82

    The Story of Coca-Cola

9. Making Giant Changes 94

    The Story of the Total Lifestyle Change

10. Upgrading Identity..108

    The Story of 5K's

Building Resilience **119**

11. Living Life on My Terms 121

    The Story of the Bearded Man's Way of Life

12. Embracing Obstacles..134

    The Story of the Advantages

13. Diffusing Triggers..145

    The Story of Button Love

14. Joining a Growth Community 154

    The Story of Circles of Men

Doing Inner Work **175**

15. Embracing Myself 177

    The Story of My Frenchness

16. Uncovering and Changing Hidden Beliefs..........188

    The Story of the Four Women

17. Transforming Life Completely.............................197

    The Story of One Hour a Day

18. Releasing Shame 207

    The Story of Interviewing

19. Listening to My Inner Voice 216

    The Story of Landing My Dream Job

Sun, Love, and Living from the Heart 231

What it Means to Live From The Heart 237

Afterword 243

Acknowledgments 247

Emails 249

Preface

"If you want to cure the world, don't emanate fear, emanate love." - Ram Dass

I've always known I'd write a book about my life someday.

In 2019, I felt that someday was now. So, before work, I'd set the timer for 20 minutes and write stories from my life. Whatever stories I was inspired or compelled to write.

Days of writing turned into weeks. Weeks turned into months. Some stories I had shared with others. Most I hadn't.

Some stories were fun and exciting to write down. They brought a smile to my face.

Some stories were hard to write down. They brought a tear or two to my face.

Some stories surprised me. I felt trepidation about anyone else reading them.

By the end of 2019, I felt a sense of completion. So, I put the stories in one document and read them one by one.

After reading them all, I had a flash of inspiration. I now knew exactly what the theme of my memoir would be and how I'd divide the book. I also knew which story would be the first story.

I worked through over half a dozen drafts for the next three years. I worked on shaping these stories and lessons into a coherent, meaningful book.

Working on these stories helped me understand much more about my choices and their impact on my life. It also helped me make peace with much of what I went through.

But for years, I didn't have a title that satisfied me.

Finally, in early 2023, I started working with a graphic designer to create a book cover. A book cover needs a title.

I meditated deeply on the subject. As I closed my eyes and got still, the title "Learning to Live from the Heart" eventually came to me. It wasn't a title I had considered before.

I could tell the title would fit with the flash of inspiration I had received years earlier. It fits the theme of my memoir.

At first, I resisted the title. I'm not perfect at living from the heart. I've failed a lot. I do succeed a lot more now than I used to. But I still have moments when I'm not. Who was I to title my memoir as such?

However, as I worked through the resistance, I realized that's why I have the word "Learning" in the title. Because I've made it my mission to learn to live from the heart for the past 10+ years. And I'll continue learning for the rest of my life.

Living from the heart is an ideal. One in which we humans can perhaps never always be perfect. But it's an ideal that we can aim for. By focusing on this ideal, we improve ourselves. Our experience of life improves. We also have a more positive impact on others and the world. That's what I've experienced in my own life.

The goal of learning to live from the heart isn't to be better than others or to live up to some kind of ideal that other people or society has for us. Instead, it's to work continuously to better align ourselves with the universal principle of love. To align our physical human nature as best we can with that energy that flows through our hearts, through us, and through the universe. It's to be better at it today than yesterday. And to be better at it tomorrow than we are today.

Once I accepted that title for my memoir, I went through a few more rounds of editing my book's stories. I also sent my book to test readers (some might call them beta readers), got their feedback, and made extensive updates to it.

Rather than arranging the stories chronologically, I've arranged them by sections. Each section has a theme. Within the sections, the stories are generally (but not always) set chronologically by the start date. There can be a lot of overlap in the time frame between each story. However, each chapter is its own story and can stand alone.

I've ended up dividing all of my story chapters into three parts. The first part is the story. The second part is called "My Reflection." Introspection has been crucial in my growth. Thus, I reflect on the story and what I've learned. The last part is called "Your Reflection". This memoir is about consciously growing. Therefore, I offer questions to help you grow through your own introspection. I'd suggest writing the answers on paper or electronically for the best results. Answering these questions is of course optional, though I think taking the time to answer them will be beneficial.

I've written each story to be as accurate as possible. There are no "composite characters" or "composite events". Each event happened as best as I can recall. I also examined my journal entries to ensure that the stories were as accurate a recollection as possible. However, this book is about my life, not about the lives of others. I've chosen to be public about these stories, but

3

others haven't. Thus, I have taken steps to preserve other people's privacy and identity. In that aim, I have changed some data related to some people's identities, such as names and other identifying information.

Chapter 1

Deciding to Align With Love
The Story of the Green Wig

One day, I wore a green wig. It changed everything for me.

It was St. Patrick's Day, 2008. I was 31 years old. In the United States, it is common to see some people wear green clothing, including green wigs, at St. Patrick's Day Parades.

However, on that day, I wasn't in the United States. I was in France.

France doesn't celebrate Saint Patrick's Day. No one wore a green wig on that day except for me. Despite my intense fear of what people would think of me, I was wearing one for my first time.

No one else around me seemed to know it was Saint Patrick's Day. Except for the woman walking with me as we crossed the crowded city center. She knew it was St. Patrick's Day. However, she wasn't wearing a green wig. She was wearing a bright pink wig.

That day was the first day we met. Her name was Josephine, and I had fallen head over heels in love with her.

Origin

Six months earlier, I was sitting in my work office at the headquarters of an independent oil company in Oklahoma. I had been working there for a few months. I also moved in with my mother to save money for graduate school.

Life felt like walking through a haunted horror house with ghosts and monsters coming from all sides. I was doing my best to avoid all of them by staying in a small corner. It was hard and scary to venture out.

I had graduated from college seven years earlier, full of hope and aspiration to impact the world. Instead, I had failed dramatically. I ended up being unemployed for a little while. I finally worked at a retail store for four years, feeling stuck there. Finally, I got out of retail by working at the headquarters of an oil company. While the oil company job wasn't bad, it wasn't how I wanted to impact the world.

My life wasn't working. It was a complete mess. I was living a shadow of what I knew I could be living. I started spending a lot of time on an online personal development forum to explore how I could grow. I wanted to find answers to life's vexing problems and create a life I'd love to live.

Josephine

Josephine was a participant in that online forum, too. She was a few years younger than me. I saw the pictures she posted online. She had blond hair and was beautiful.

She once wrote a post about her insecurities regarding her appearance. So, Josephine then posted unflattering pictures of herself online as a way to stop caring about what people thought of her looks.

Josephine also feared a dark alley near her place. So, she walked at night, alone, in that alley with all her strength and power. Foolish? Perhaps. But courageous.

Josephine had a public blog where she wrote revealingly about what she was going through and learning. Sometimes, she received nasty comments. When that happened, I didn't see her take it personally. She once told me that when someone is hostile toward her because of what she writes, it has nothing to do with her. It has everything to do with their inner conflict and issues. She had compassion for those individuals.

I found her bold as hell. Incredibly courageous and so heart-centered.

Witnessing her in action on the forum stirred something profound within me. I felt a longing within me that had long been suppressed. Maybe I didn't have to be closed off and isolated from the world. Maybe I didn't have to have my heart closed off. Perhaps I didn't have to live in fear.

I wrote her a message: "Hi Josephine, I'm curious about…". I don't remember what it was that I was curious about. She replied. We casually exchanged messages for a while.

As we started exchanging longer and longer messages and chatted in real time, I decided to do something entirely new for me. I chose to be fully honest and transparent with Josephine about everything that came up in our conversations.

I was on the forum to grow, not to pick up a woman. I knew that to succeed in my growth, I needed to speak the truth and not try to impress anyone. With Josephine, I told the complete truth about myself, not hiding anything that would reflect poorly on me.

Amazingly, she responded with acceptance. We started spending so much time communicating via written messages and voice chat. I told her one day I was attracted to her. She replied she was attracted to me too. We hadn't met yet, but we started experiencing an online romantic relationship.

One weekend, we decided to take a break from texting and chatting. Everything was going great; we had been communicating so much that we needed rest.

That Saturday night, I became angry at my mother. Then, that evening, I received a message from Josephine. She wrote, "Hey, I know we're not supposed to message this weekend, but I'm getting a strong feeling of you being angry. Is everything ok?"

I was stunned. This woman I hadn't met in person could sense my feelings even when we were not communicating! I can't hide my emotions from this woman.

Until then, I hid most of my emotions from my partners and even myself. But now I knew I couldn't do that with Josephine. So, for the first time ever, I became emotionally open with another human being. Amazingly, Josephine accepted me with my emotions.

The result was the start of a connection unlike anything I had previously experienced. Because Josephine accepted me, I felt free to be myself, share, and learn about myself through our ever-deepening conversations.

I felt understood, respected, and loved. I started being in that blissful state of falling in love with her.

One day, I wrote to her:

"Josephine, I want to come and meet you,"

"OK, you can come and stay at my place," she wrote back.

One little hiccup.

I was in Oklahoma. She was in the south of France. Over five thousand miles away. Fortunately, I was also French. I had family in France.

So, I booked a flight to France to visit my family in Normandy. While there, I planned to take a 12-hour train ride from Paris to see Josephine. I realized I would arrive at Josephine's city on St. Patrick's Day. Josephine found it fun when I explained what St. Patrick's Day meant in the US.

As we talked about it, we wondered what if we both wore wigs on the day of the meeting. She could wear a pink wig she had. I could wear a green wig I'd buy in the store before flying over.

Until our conversation, I had never contemplated wearing a wig for anything. What would people think? I had it ingrained in me that only crazy and degenerate people had colored hair! I had lived my life doing my best to avoid doing anything potentially embarrassing or socially scary. Yet here I was, contemplating wearing a wig in public. It had until then been far beyond the realm of possibilities for me to risk such judgments. My body would freeze to stop me.

However, I was in love with Josephine and felt inspired by her courage. It seems like an exciting idea. So, I bought a wig shaped like a golf hat with wild green hair coming out in the middle.

Meeting

On St. Patrick's Day, the train pulled into the station in the small city of Perpignan in the south of France. I put on my green wig. I grabbed my backpack and made my way to the exit doors. Once on the platform, I looked around at a sea of faces.

Then I saw her. She was the only person in the crowd wearing a pink wig. She had a big smile on her face. I also had a big smile too.

After we greeted each other, we started walking toward her place to drop off my backpack. While we walked and talked, I kept my eyes glued to her. I didn't want to risk seeing anyone else's disapproving looks at my wig. That would ruin everything. I drew strength from staying focused on her.

We spent one blissful week together.

I saw how Josephine lived with courage and love toward me, other people, and animals. She showed me a way to live I had never experienced before, a way to live with courage and heart, one that I yearned with my entire body, compassion, and soul to live. While with her, I lived that way.

After that week, it was time for me to return to my family in Normandy, followed by a return to the US.

I planned on seeing her again. I never did, not in person.

A month after my return from France, I was at work. Things were going well between us two. I planned to return to France in the summer to spend more time with her.

A message from her on Google Chat came up.

"Hey, are you free to talk?" she wrote. I said, "Yeah."

Josephine then wrote that a man from her past had returned. She wanted to explore a relationship with him. She was breaking up with me.

Tears rolled down my cheek.

"Ok, I understand."

I thought I'd be ok. I had always been ok during breakups with other women.

But I wasn't ok. I felt devastated. My life was crumbling, and my world turned upside down. Even breathing was painful.

I had spent the last seven years trying my best to navigate this scary life path. I tried to avoid the threatening ghosts and monsters around me as much as possible.

During my time with Josephine, I experienced what it was like to live a courageous, heart-centered life. To do things because my heart desired them. Instead of doing things out of fear.

Kissing her that first night while wearing my green wig symbolized what it was like to live that courageous, heart-centered life.

My hopes - no, my plans - no, my desperate desire was that by spending as much time with her as possible, I could grow to be that courageous, heart-centered individual.

But she had broken up with me.

The Decision

Within a couple of weeks after the breakup, I read an article online called "The Rise of the Lightworker" by Steve Pavlina. The article stressed the importance of living from the heart and aligning with love. That would help to combat the darkness and fearmongering in the world. The world needed more heart-centered and love-centered people than ever.

After reading it, I felt inspired. I wanted my life to make an impact. I decided that, Josephine or not, I would commit to living from the heart. Instead of living a life based on fear (either the avoidance or the use of it), I'd commit to living a life where I would act based on love.

I would stop shrinking to a small corner, hoping nothing would hurt me. Instead, I wanted to live a life in which I venture out of that corner, face those ghosts and monsters, and aim to do the greatest good for humanity.

I devoted myself to doing whatever it took to grow into that heart-centered vision I had for myself, my life, and my idea of how the world could be.

Why?

Because having tasted the fruits briefly, there was no going back. There was no putting the genie back in the bottle. There was no forgetting what I had experienced.

But this was more than just about me. It was about the world. About humanity. About life as a whole.

The alternative to living from the heart is to cede the world to be ruled by those who use fear, harvest fear, and unleash it onto others. This leads people to live deeply unfulfilled robotic lives. Lives that are far from what they could be. Lives that are disconnected. In essence, the way I had been living.

But worst, those who rule with fear use fear to hurt people. Hurt emotionally. Hurt mentally. And hurt physically either directly or through threats of physical violence.

If the world is to have an answer to this madness of violence, it is not by becoming more fear-based than the next person. It is not by committing or threatening more violence than the next person. It is not by closing oneself off from the heart even more.

The way out of being ruled by fear is to become heart-centered as individuals. To use love as a guide, light, and compass. To do all we can to become courageous enough to live a heart-centered life, with love and respect. A life of caring deeply. Not just about ourselves and our loved ones but for others on this planet.

It is about doing our part to help create a world ruled by the heart, love, respect, and compassion. A world where heart-based principled leaders naturally rise to lead. A world where people can be their highest selves, free from the shackles of being ruled by fear, self-imposed restrictions, and blind adherence to outdated and toxic ways of being.

Regardless of my role in the world, I wanted to do my part as a man to become heart-centered. My part is to inoculate myself against fear-based rulers. And to do good in the world.

This is what I committed myself to. I didn't know how I would do it. But I knew this was my path, purpose, and way forward. I would try my best.

My Reflection

I knew it wouldn't be easy. I couldn't just flip a switch and instantly become this new person. I had spent decades living by running away from fears, living without trust, and operating from a place outside my heart.

To become heart-centered and live from love, I'd have to let go of most of my existing tools, comfortable way of living, and most of what I knew how to do. I would need to learn a new way of living.

I'd be so out of my comfort zone. I knew I'd make mistakes. But that's a normal part of doing new things.

I had a dream soon after the decision. In my dream, I had just finished talking to Josephine, and she announced she was breaking up with me. Then, after the news, I set out to walk through a long mansion in the dark. I was on my own, without friends or family to help me. I felt scared walking through this long, dark path by myself. The dream foreshadowed what I would go through over the next few years.

Nevertheless, I committed myself to this decision. I would do my best to implement this decision over the next 10 years.

Your Reflection

Have you ever met someone or spent time with someone who showed you a whole new way to experience life, a life that you would love to live?

What qualities of that person did you admire that you wished you exhibited more?

How much time do you live from the heart and aligned with love?
How much of your time do you live in fear or aligned with fear?

How do you feel about your answer?

Facing Fears

"Do one thing every day that scares you."

Eleanor Roosevelt

Chapter 2

What I Fear, I Must Do
The Story of Free Hugs

A few months after the Green Wig event, I saw a video of a man standing on the side of a street holding a sign with the words "Free Hugs." Total strangers walked toward him, extended their arms, and hugged him.

"What audacity!" I thought.

The man, through hugs, created a connection with random men, women, and people of all types! That seemed fascinating but also terrifying. No way I could do it, I thought. I lived an almost hug-less life and couldn't contemplate hugging so many people. Hugging also wasn't part of my French culture. And forget about asking for hugs while holding a big sign that says "Free Hugs." What kind of rejection would I be facing? A lot, probably!

What I fear, I must do

When I decided to learn to live from the heart, I thought about the mindset of "What I fear, I must do." I had first heard of this mindset about eight years earlier. I thought then it was stupid. I wanted to avoid fear; not create more anxiety by doing scary stuff!

However, by 2008, I realized the cost of running away from fear. Looking back over the last eight years, I could see that my life had shrunk significantly. By avoiding scary things, my comfort zone had shrunk over time until it became tiny.

Despite my fears of doing a Free Hugs event, I could see an inkling of desire like a ray of sunlight piercing the stormy clouds.

If I was going to start living from the heart, I had the sense that I needed to stop running away from what I feared. To stop acting like a coward. Instead, I needed to do what I feared for the simple reason that I feared it. The idea was that by doing what I feared, I'd eventually no longer fear it. Instead of my world shrinking, my world would then expand.

Those words sounded nice, but could I do that? Could I do what I feared for the simple reason that I feared it? That seemed like a tall order.

However, I sensed that my success in learning to live from the heart and align with love rested on being able to do what I feared.

Meeting Free Huggers

After, I moved from Oklahoma to Las Vegas to attend graduate school. I searched online for a "Free Hugs" group in Las Vegas.

On November 6th, I drove to a "Free Hugs" sign-making meeting. It was held inside a Mexican restaurant. I saw a dozen people sitting at multiple tables as I entered the restaurant. However, instead of food and drinks on the table, I saw white poster boards and colored markers. I also noticed a few white poster boards on another otherwise empty table with the words "Free Hugs" written in bright colors. I also felt the energy of excitement as these people were making Free Hugs signs.

I introduced myself and sat with them. They seemed friendly and welcoming. I then took a white poster board and some colored markers. I used the markers to write "Free Hugs" on several poster boards. I felt excited.

The following day, I drove back to the restaurant. The plan: Walk with the group to the Las Vegas Strip, a few minutes away. Then, hold the "Free Hugs" sign in front of the casinos.

As I parked my car, my pulse began to quicken. Once I walked inside the restaurant, I saw many people talking with each other. They seemed excited about going outside to hold the Free Hugs signs. However, I started to feel a rise of panic inside me. These thoughts rapidly went through my mind: *"What the hell am I doing here? This is madness. Get out! This is dangerous! Walk away!"*. I felt a sinking feeling in the pit of my stomach.

Without saying a word to anyone, I got up, walked to my car, and went straight home. There was no way I was going to do this Free Hug thing.

In my journal that evening, I wrote down the following:

> *"I went to the hug thingy and ended up walking. I felt too uncomfortable. I felt scared...There is something in me that is against giving free hugs to strangers. I wanted to do it because it'd be a sign of courage, but I'm not ready to develop that kind of courage yet. I thought it'd be easy with a group, but no, even with a group, it's still something I have to do alone - as I'm alone with that sign. Maybe it's related to rejection. Maybe it's related to actually giving hugs. Do I like giving hugs? I give and get so few hugs. Since in Vegas, I've gotten 2 hugs - both from the same person. Before that, I'd live without*

giving anyone hugs - I probably spent the whole year without giving hugs at all to anyone."

Observing

Over the next few months, I made several more reservations online to attend a "Free Hugs" event. However, each time, I found an excuse not to go.

Why should I try again? It was scary as hell. The mantra came back to mind. "What I fear, I must do." I feared the Free Hugs; therefore, I needed to do it for no reason other than that. If I would grow and live from the heart, I needed to become comfortable doing what I feared.

I then thought: What if I just observed the "Free Hugs" event without picking up a sign? Maybe that would help me get more comfortable?

Soon after, I drove to one of the "Free Hugs" events on the Las Vegas Strip. From a distance, I saw about five people holding signs.

As I walked toward them, those familiar panic feelings began. My thoughts rushed uncontrollably. *"Get out of here! If you stand next to them, it'll look like I am with them! I can't do that! This is too dangerous!"*

I turned around, returned to my car, and drove home.

I felt dejected. But then I thought, okay, at least I had gotten closer to the Free Huggers than I did before. Obviously, I feared the Free Hugs. How could I overcome this?

Soon after, I ran into the organizer of the "Free Hugs" event while attending a non-related meeting. I told him of my struggles and my desire. He listened and responded with compassion. He invited me to join him at a "Free Hug" event and observe.

On February 14th, I drove to the Las Vegas Paris Casino to observe a "Free Hugs" event. I parked my car and began walking toward the event. I checked myself. No uncontrollable racing thoughts. No sense of panic in me. Good. Apparently, talking to the organizer about my fears had helped a lot. I kept walking.

I approached seven people holding "Free Hugs" signs on the sidewalk. The organizer welcomed me to observe them. He gave me his camera and asked me to take pictures. Perfect. I felt like I was part of the event…without being a part of the event.

For the next two hours, I saw countless people hugging. I saw smiles on so many people's faces. There was so much joy, laughter, and warmth. I found myself laughing out of joy as well.

After an hour of observing, I hugged each of the seven people holding a "Free Hug" sign. It was fun. I received more hugs at that event than I had the entire previous year from anyone I hadn't dated.

After two more hours of observing, I decided to stand between two of the people holding a sign. I raised a sign above my head. A man saw me and came by and hugged me. Then, a woman came by and hugged me. Those hugs felt nice.

After a few minutes, one of the sign holders beside me walked away to take a break. Once that happened, that familiar fear returned. The thought, *"Who the hell am I to hold that sign,"* flashed through my mind. I put the sign down and walked away.

While I only held the sign briefly, I had now tasted, albeit briefly, the sweet success of holding the sign. I wanted more. Way more.

Holding the Sign

While I had made progress, I still had problems holding that sign. I pondered how to overcome the resistance.

About a week later, I had a couple of insights.

First, I realized one of my beliefs was, "Everything must be earned." One of my family members impressed that upon me when I was growing up. I felt hugs had to be "earned." Who was I to "earn" a hug from total strangers without even talking with them?

To deal with this, I decided that a hug did not have to be "earned." A hug benefits both people. I decided that I was there to give hugs to people, not to receive something "unearned." It was a slight distinction but a crucial one.

Second, I realized I was still feeling so much fear of being rejected. So, I thought I could try to visualize feeling unconditionally loved while holding that "Free Hugs Sign." Maybe I wouldn't fear rejection if I felt loved unconditionally? Almost every free moment I had for the next few days; I visualized holding that sign while feeling unconditionally loved.

Ten days after my previous episode of observing, I planned on showing up at the next "Free Hugs" event. That event would be held just a hundred yards south of the Paris Casino. Two hours before the event, I felt nervous. But at the same time, I felt that it'd be all right. I wasn't panicking. My thoughts weren't darting and racing. I stayed calm.

After parking my car, I walked out to the area of the Free Hugs event. There, I saw three men holding a sign. I greeted them by hugging them. I saw the Paris Casino with its Eiffel Tower a hundred yards away as I looked around. Across the streets I saw the majestic fountain of the Bellagio Casino. A steady stream of people walked by. Cars zipped by us on the streets and people were talking as they walked. I also heard people's excitement at seeing the Free Hugs sign. It felt like such a festive mood as people were walking around with their drinks or cameras in their hands

I removed my jacket by placing it on the ground a couple yards away. Then, I grabbed a "Free Hugs" sign and faced the crowd. While consciously choosing to feel unconditionally loved, I raised the sign above my head. I was relieved that instead of panicking, I felt calm.

Soon, a passer-by walked over to me with a smile and hugged me. That was a lovely hug, and I felt excited at having received it. After the hug, I raised my sign back up. Then, another person with a smile came to hug me. They wanted to take a picture of us two, so we posed.

By then, I didn't have to focus on feeling unconditionally loved. I felt that sense of universal love from the hugs. People came by to receive their hugs. They were all ages, from the old to the young, from men to women, from people walking by themselves to people in groups taking turns to hug me. I saw a couple of tough, macho biker-looking dudes break out a big smile upon seeing the signs and coming to get their hugs. I saw a car stop by the side of the road, and then several young women jumped out. They ran over to get hugs and then ran back into the car.

Many people took pictures. When they did, I asked them to photograph us with my camera. There was a lot of laughter and joy.

After one hug, a man put a dollar bill on the jacket I had laid down. Before I had a chance to protest, the man moved on. I moved my jacket farther away since I meant it to be "Free Hugs," not "Hugs for donation.". I later thought how awesome it was that I was facing my fears and connecting with people, and someone wanted to pay me for that!

The other sign holders took a break. I was then all alone, holding the sign. I felt completely comfortable with that.

In the three hours I held the sign, I hugged more people than I had in the preceding eight years, if not my entire life.

I noticed many people were walking by without stopping for a hug. I saw how more people walked by than came to get a hug from me. Yet, I didn't feel rejected. My sign never stayed up long without receiving and giving a hug.

After it was over, I realized how warm and connected I felt. I sensed how hugging is a recognition of our shared humanity. It's also a recognition of the love that flows in the universe. I felt incredibly touched by the experience.

I also felt proud I had finally succeeded in doing what I feared. I had grown my courage. I also successfully applied the mantra "What I feared, I must do." Now, I was a step closer to living more from the heart.

My Reflection

Doing the things I feared brought a temporary heightened state of fear, but it was a controlled fear. It was the fear of being courageous rather than the fear of cowardice. I liked that much better.

I learned that some fears were too big to tackle all at once. Baby steps needed to be taken first. The Free Hugs was like that for me. But I didn't know that until I had tried it.

What I loved about the mantra "What I fear I must do" is that it cuts away all the inner chatter about whether I should do it. Instead of spending energy debating whether I should do it, I could instead start applying my energy to figuring out how I could do it.

I've also realized I tended to fear doing those things that part of me had a desire to do. Those things I had no fear of doing—like crossing a busy street with my eyes closed—are things no part of me desired to do. So, if I feared doing something, it indicated that parts of me desired to do it.

How could I know the benefit of doing something I feared that I've never done? I don't. But that fear indicated that a part of me feels pulled to do it. Thus, I might as well try it out and experience the benefits firsthand. At the very least, I'll grow my courage doing it.

I found that courage was like a muscle. The more it got used, the stronger it grew. Thus, I developed my courage muscles by doing the things I feared. That then allowed me to face more fears. Overall, that enhanced my life and enabled me to live more from the heart. It also made me more immune to other people who tried to use fear to motivate or manipulate me.

During the eight years before I started applying the mantra "What I fear I must do," my life shrank significantly. Conversely, my life expanded so much eight years after using that mantra. My life became almost unrecognizable compared to its previous life, in a good way.

Your Reflection

What is an action that you feel a desire to do and also feel a fear of doing it?

Has your life shrunk or expanded in the last 10 years? Have you systematically faced your fears? Or have you been running away from them?

What kind of life do you get to live now as a result?

Chapter 3

Making a Game Out of It
The Story of the Hugging Contest

"Can I give you a hug?"

A 30-year-old man with wild brown hair and a European accent asked me that question. We had just met while standing at a Las Vegas casino court. We both attended a meet and greet for a three-day personal development workshop starting the next day.

"Why?" I thought, *"I don't have my 'Free Hugs' sign up!"*

While I had hugged hundreds of people during the "Free Hugs" event seven months earlier, I still rarely hugged people. It felt awkward.

I didn't want to say "yes," but I said it anyway. The "no" wasn't strong enough in me to refuse. We hugged. It was an awkward hug. The man looked at me afterward with a puzzled look. He had probably seen me write about the Free Hugs I did and wondered why I didn't hug him well.

That was my introduction to Daan Buckinx, who would inspire me to complete my revolution with hugging. Little did we know then that despite being only 30 years old, he didn't have much time to live.

Daan had flown in from Belgium to attend the three-day workshop in Las Vegas. Like France, Belgium doesn't have a hugging culture. However, Daan wanted to explore hugging fully.

Daan's Speed-Hugging

On the first day of the workshop, during one of the sessions where participants could share their thoughts or questions with the group, Daan stood up to share. He declared that his goal was to hug total strangers as fast as possible. He wondered how long an interaction would be needed before he could hug someone.

During the workshop breaks, I saw him walking around the casino. He approached many strangers to talk with them and eventually hugged them.

At the start of the second day, he stood up again during a sharing session at the workshop. He reported excitedly, "It's now only taking me one minute of talking before getting to hug!" He said that inside elevators, he'd start talking with people. Then, he'd hug them as the door opened before they left. After celebrating that win with us, he continued experimenting some more.

At the end of the second day, he announced, "It's now taking only 10 seconds of talking before I get to the hug!"

By the end of the third day of the workshop, he proudly stood up and said, "I can now hug total strangers instantly without talking!" Daan reported making eye contact with strangers, smiling big, opening his arms wide, and people would come and hug him.

After the workshop, he stayed in Las Vegas for a few more days before returning to Belgium. He wrote about how he estimated he had hugged 400 people during his week-long stay in Las Vegas.

I was impressed. Despite Daan coming from the same culture of non-hugging that I did, he had been able to welcome hugging into his life so fast. I saw how much warmth and love he spread with these hugs.

I had done the "Free Hugs" campaign but still had difficulties hugging without holding a sign. It was so out of my comfort zone.

After the workshop, I asked the presenter if I could volunteer at the next workshop. He said that he had noticed I had difficulties hugging people. He wanted to maintain the warm, connecting atmosphere of the workshop. Therefore, he wanted his volunteers to be available to embrace those who wanted to hug. Thus, I wouldn't be a good candidate to volunteer.

I realized he was right. But more than that, I realized I no longer wanted barriers to hugging people. Instead, I wanted to be more like Daan.

How could I overcome this challenge of hugging people one-on-one without a sign?

The Contest

The answer to that came from my friend Boniebelle, an American living in Europe. She flew to the US three months later to attend a personal development workshop I would also be attending.

Boniebelle and I discussed my issue and desire to overcome my hesitation and resistance to hugging. Together, we came up with the idea of hugging as many people as possible at the workshop. What if we made it a contest between her and me? Like me,

Boniebelle had done a Free Hug event in Europe. We thought it'd be exciting. Unlike Daan, who aimed to hug people outside the workshop, Bonniebelle and I figured we'd just stick to hugging people who attended the workshop. For fun, we set a prize for the winner: they would receive a shoulder massage from the other.

How would I do in the contest? Bonniebelle seemed to have an easier time hugging people than I did. But if I could go all out, that could help me overcome my resistance and remaining fears regarding hugging. I'd then be able to live more from the heart. The thought of what Daan had done kept me inspired.

As soon as the first day of the workshop started, all of my hesitation and fears about hugging people immediately disappeared. I was on a mission. Nothing would keep me from winning. I approached people, disregarded any resistance or fears I felt, and asked to hug them.

I'd ask them during breaks and breakout sessions. I'd ask each day before the workshop started and after it ended. They all seem to welcome it. Some of them enjoyed it very much. They gave wonderful hugs back.

Seeing Boniebelle hugging people fueled my desire to find more people to hug.

By the end of the workshop, I had hugged almost all 100 attendees. When Boniebelle and I compared our numbers, I won the competition!

That experience completely changed my relationship with hugging. Whatever hesitation and fears I had about embracing were now gone. I now quickly hugged people and welcomed hugs. My connection to others and ability to live from the heart had just made a giant leap.

Later that year, I met up with a man I hadn't seen in over ten years. The man and I had never hugged before. However, as soon as he saw me, he asked if he could hug me. I warmly welcomed it. I doubt that would have happened if I still had that resistance to being embraced.

Years later, I worked for a spiritual center. For years, I would joyfully receive 30-40 hugs each week. That also would not have been possible had I not overcome my previous blocks and fears.

Postscript: Daan Buckinx

I kept in touch with Daan Buckinx. He returned to Las Vegas a year later to attend the same workshop. I also participated in that workshop. We had a great time reconnecting. I told him how he had inspired me on my hugging journey.

Daan had developed cancer despite being only 31 years old. Due to his chemotherapy, he had lost his wild brown hair and was now bald.

Despite his treatment, he continued to be inspiring and incredibly loving. He wanted to love people as much as he could. As a result, he left behind a powerful sense of connection and love during this trip.

The following year, I sensed his death was near. I sent him my last message to let him know how much I appreciated him and how much he had inspired me. Not long afterward, he died at age 32.

My Reflection

I was so glad I got to meet Daan and spend time with him. He touched and inspired my life, as well as many others. His death reminded me of how important it was for me to overcome my fears. And to overcome whatever may hold me back from living fully in my heart. One day, my time will also be over. Before that happens, I want to have lived as fully as possible.

I learned from this experience that growth may not be linear. I may have felt pulled to overcome a fear (such as the Free Hugs), and it felt like a mountain to climb. Once I'd climbed that mountain, I could then see another mountain to climb on. For example, being more like Daan and hugging people more freely. I learned that I often can't see the next mountain unless I climb that first mountain. That's ok. What mattered was that I kept climbing those new mountains as they appeared. That I continued doing those things I feared to keep moving forward. That helped me continue learning to live more from my heart.

Here are ways I found to make growth a fun game:

- Competing with someone I have a genuine friendship with or someone that I like and respect.
- Keeping it fun and lighthearted.
- Keeping track of the score in a concrete way. I used to keep track of it on paper but keeping it on a cloud-based spreadsheet or the notes function on a smartphone also worked.
- Setting a fun reward for winning.
- Supporting each other to do our best. While it's a competition, my attitude is that while I'll do my best to win, I also want the other person to do well and grow from it.

Setting up games on my own can be a fun way to motivate me to grow. For example, getting rejected x number of times when I worked on facing the fear of rejection. I rewarded myself when I reached the score I aimed for.

Your Reflection

Have you ever received kind and compassionate feedback from someone that you then used to help fuel your growth?

Have you ever used a fun contest to help you overcome a fear or resistance?

Chapter 4

Staying Connected Despite the Fear
The Story of Public Speaking

One day, as a high school senior, I was called to the principal's office. No, I wasn't in trouble. Instead, the principal asked me to give a speech during the graduation ceremony. That's what you get at my high school if your GPA is in the top four of the graduating class.

Just the thought of it gave me butterflies. I'd have to speak in the High School Gym, facing 220 graduating seniors and 800 family members for an audience of over 1,000. I told the principal I'd need to think about it.

As I pondered it over the following week, I felt afraid at the idea of giving such a speech. What would happen to me on stage, in front of this many people? I was reassured by what the principal said about the support I'd have to help me prepare.

A few days later, I returned to the principal's office. I agreed to give the speech. I felt it was important to go through the process and do my best. He told me that in all of his years of experience, that was the first time he thought a student might decline.

For the next few months, I met weekly with the other students who were also giving speeches at graduation. In addition to the four of us with the top GPA, two of the elected officers of the senior student body would also be giving a speech. We met with a teacher assigned to help us prepare.

Together, we wrote each of our respective speech word for word. We incorporated what we each wanted to say, plus we received a lot of feedback from the teacher on what we could or could not say. We labored over every single word in the speech. We also started practicing with each other.

Outside of the meetings, I often visualized that the speech would go well. I'd close my eyes and see myself on stage speaking well and the words coming out well. I was training myself through the power of visualization. I was still nervous, but it was manageable.

Two days before the ceremony, I wondered, "Am I going to do this? Stand in front of 1,000 people and speak?"

The day before graduation, all 220 graduating seniors gathered in the gym to practice for the ceremony. Without the families present, we practiced giving our speech to the seniors. That went well. I felt ok that I could do this.

Then, the next day, over 1,000 people filled up the gym. It was full. I had my graduation gown and cap on, as did all graduating seniors. I sat on stage in front of everyone while waiting for my turn. I watched the other speakers go up to the podium, face the 1,000 people in the high school gym, and give their speeches. I felt a little nervous. But I also felt fully prepared.

When it was my turn, I stood up and walked to the podium. My heart beat a little faster. The moment I had been visualizing for months was now here. I took out the notecards with my speech written out. I looked around and saw 1,000 people looking at me.

Then, I opened my mouth to start my speech. Before I could say that first word, the tassel attached to the top of my graduating cap flew straight into my mouth. The crowd erupted in laughter. I smiled, as I found it funny. That helped me relax completely. I gave my speech without any problem and even without even feeling anxious.

Afterward, I felt proud of having risen to the occasion. I figured that meant I had mastered public speaking.

I was so wrong.

College

A few months later, I started college. In my first quarter, I received an assignment to present in one of my classes. There were only 20 students in the class. Since I had given a speech to 1,000 people, I figured that addressing 20 students should be simple.

It wasn't.

Two days before the speech, my stomach started feeling pain from the fear. My body ached. I was so nervous.

On the day of the speech, I walked to the podium. My knees shook. My stomach was in pain. My voice was uneven and quivered. I barely mumbled what I had to say. I don't think anyone understood a word.

When I sat down, I was a nervous wreck. Giving a speech to 20 people had been more nerve-wracking than 1,000 people!

Why?

I later realized that for the previous speech, I had a support group of teachers and fellow students whom I met with every week for several months. Every word of my address was crafted carefully. I also spent much time visualizing the speech. I had been part of a well-oiled machine.

For the second speech, I had none of that. It was just me, terrified of public speaking and speaking alone without support.

College Public Speaking Class

A few years later, I registered for a public speaking class as an elective in college. I wanted to get a better handle on public speaking. It was still terrifying me too much. I needed to overcome that.

I showed up to the first day's class. The teacher explained the four graded speeches we'd have to give. I couldn't imagine submitting myself to that kind of torture. So, right after that first class, I dropped it.

Near the end of the semester, I felt bummed out that I had dropped the class. I felt a renewed sense of how it was vital to overcome this fear of public speaking.

So, the next semester, I registered for the public speaking class again. After a few weeks, I gave my first prepared speech. Preparing for it took so much energy out of me. I had been a nervous wreck preparing for it. After that speech, I couldn't imagine putting myself through what felt like torture again three more times.

So, I went to the registration office and dropped the class. I felt dejected.

The following semester, I wanted to try again. I felt how important it was to overcome this fear. This time, though, I felt determined to do what it took to complete that class. Thus, I signed up for the public speaking class for the third time.

I threw myself fully into the class. Gave all four prepared speeches. I got an "A" in the class. I finally passed a public speaking class after three attempts! I felt happy.

I learned a lot about giving speeches. But I knew I wasn't done.

Toastmasters

The class's teacher recommended I start attending a local Toastmasters club. Toastmasters clubs were a way for people to practice giving speeches to each other. They were made up of about 20 members who usually met weekly.

I found one to join. The club was full of professionals while I was still a student. I was assigned a mentor, someone who worked at NASA. She helped me prepare for my first speech. I felt so incredibly nervous giving that first speech. It was hard. But I made it through.

Over the next two years, I attended the club's meeting almost every week. I gave many impromptu speeches (called Table Topics). That was when I'd be asked a question and would have two minutes to answer the question without any preparation. I enjoyed those a lot as I got to be creative on the spot. And if I stumbled, it didn't matter. Everyone knew I had no time to prepare.

However, giving formal, prepared speeches was a different story. I had my second prepared speech ready. However, I felt terrified about giving the speech once I arrived at the meeting. I went to the bathroom and almost threw up. I backed out of giving that speech. Somehow, I found it much harder to give prepared speeches to a group of professionals than to give speeches to fellow students.

As a result, despite attending about 100 meetings over two years, I only gave two prepared speeches. After college, I moved out of town and stopped going to Toastmasters.

Toastmasters Reloaded

Five years later, now back in town, I visited my former club. I felt scared of being there. I hadn't given a speech in years. I mentioned that to a member. He replied and reminded me that facing and overcoming our fears is essential.

I thought about it and realized he was right. I thought about how I had dealt with this fear of public speaking for seven to eight years. I had made some good progress but still had so much more to go. I decided, let's go all out! I felt determination. I thus rejoined the club.

Instead of giving two speeches every two years, like the first time in Toastmasters, I decided to give as many speeches as possible. Do it repeatedly until I get better and/or figure out a way to be calm while giving them. This meant I might have to give many bad speeches in the meantime. So be it!

Soon after I rejoined, the current president resigned mid-term. As a result, the members discussed who could take up the presidency. I spoke up and volunteered. I loved being a leader. But I also figured that being president meant being in front of the group at every meeting. What better way to overcome my fear of public speaking than having to speak every week?

I became the new president of my Toastmasters club. Not because I was any good at public speaking. But because no one else wanted to do it and,

Turns out I did love being president. I stood before the group every week and led portions of the meeting. I also started giving prepared speeches over and over as well. I tried different strategies to overcome the intense nervousness I'd feel giving those prepared speeches.

Finally, I found a solution that kept me from being a nervous mess on the platform. The solution: not give a shit about my audience. I was putting myself in a mental state where what the audience thought and felt didn't matter. The only thing that mattered was the flow of my words and ideas.

When I adopted that mental framework, I could stay centered and calm. I was able to also interact with the audience. I could read the room and update my speech in real time when I sensed a point that required elaboration or clarification.

Over the next six months, I gave more than ten formal speeches to my Toastmasters club. Sometimes, I'd be awarded the "Best Speech" award of the day. Completing the ten speeches also meant I finished the basic certification. Then, I started giving speeches to work toward my advanced certification.

I loved the feeling that I had finally conquered my fear and could give speeches comfortably. If I felt fear, I'd pump myself up Tony Robbins Style, disconnect from my audience, and speak. It would usually go well.

Graduate School

However, in 2008, I made the shift to live from the heart. How could I live from the heart and speak to an audience as if I don't care about them? How could disconnecting myself from the audience be in alignment with living with love?

I was also soon starting graduate business school and would have to make many presentations. What could I do to overcome my fears of public speaking if I couldn't disconnect from the audience? I didn't know. But I felt determined to find an answer to that problem. I wanted to be able to speak while aligned with the principle of love.

In the meantime, I decided to stop using my previous approach. I'd let myself experience whatever nervousness and fears might arise again and see what solution would emerge.

I started making presentations in my classes. My nervousness returned in force. My knees would be shaking the whole time I'd be presenting. I had a hard time standing to talk. That was painful at first.

Fortunately, it wasn't as bad as it was before. My mind was ok with the concept of giving speeches even though my body wasn't. Perhaps I had given enough speeches that my mind was ok with it even if my body wasn't.

Finally, after several presentations in which my body acted like a nervous wreck, an idea came to me. What if I used love itself? What if, while preparing for a speech, I visualized myself feeling unconditional love while giving my presentation? I used that tool for the Free Hugs events.

I tried it for an upcoming class presentation. That presentation was about business concepts. It had nothing to do with love.

However, I focused on feeling that unconditional love while giving my presentation. Success! My knees only shook briefly and then became steady for the rest of my speech. I felt confident, and I was back in command of my body.

I continued using this method to prepare myself for giving presentations during the rest of my time in business school. It worked out well.

Near the end of graduate school, I had a big speech waiting for me. It would be my most daunting and difficult speech yet. I'd speak not just to teachers and students but also to hard-core angel investors. These investors were used to grilling CEOs who solicited the investors for their money. I had seen them in action before in their investor meetings. They acted like Simon Cowell from American Idol in how verbally critical they could be. Not only would they be in the audience of my class, but they'd get to grill us with questions.

I knew from previous feedback that they wouldn't like some aspects of my presentation. I felt daunted. How can I calmly stand up before my peers and teacher, knowing these investors could be publicly critical of me?

I felt determined to make it through. So, I doubled down on visualizing feeling that unconditional love for myself as I gave that presentation.

During the presentation, the investors asked me critical questions. I responded. In front of everyone, they expressed dissatisfaction regarding part of my plan. I stayed rooted in that unconditional self-love and let what they said be brushed off.

After the speech, I sat down and took a breather. I had made it. I felt good. I felt victorious. I passed the class. I also learned and solidified a new way to give speeches while staying heart-centered and aligned with love.

My Reflection

Learning this method of imagining unconditional love before giving a speech didn't mean I never felt fear anymore. I still sometimes have felt nervous before a speech. But it meant I now had a powerful way of delivering speeches while staying aligned with love.

It had sometimes taken me years to overcome a fear. Each step forward, however, has helped. Each setback would be temporary once I stepped forward again.

Disconnecting myself from my feelings and my audience is something I had unconsciously applied to more than just public speaking. I used it in my relationships with others as well. Anytime I was afraid of something terrible happening to someone, I'd mentally disconnect myself from caring about that person. It's insidious.

Learning to stay connected to others and to what I care about despite the fear had been one of my biggest growth challenges as I learned to live more from the heart.

Your Reflection

What is a fear that has taken you years to overcome? How did you overcome it?

Do you sometimes disconnect yourself from situations or people to avoid feeling your fears? How do you feel about your answer?

Chapter 5

Diffusing the Fear
The Story of Rollercoasters

One day, as I was finishing graduate school in Las Vegas, my friend Morris said, "Let's go up on the roller coaster! It would be a great experience to face our fears".

I agreed with him. What I fear I must do.

We went to the New York New York Casino the following evening. We entered the line to buy tickets. It was a long line.

As we were standing in line to get a ticket, I noticed that my heart beat faster. My breathing became shallower. Fear was pulsating through me.

It would be my first time riding a rollercoaster since I was a teenager. I had avoided them for 10+ years.

Finally, after a long wait, Morris and I stepped into the rollercoaster car. We sat side by side.

The Ride

Once in, the roller coaster car moved slowly up a long, steep incline. I braced for what was to come as I knew we'd be thrown in all directions, including upside down. On the long, slow incline, my stomach tensed and tightened. My heart rate increased. My breathing became shallow and faster. I felt pain in the pit of my stomach. I wanted to do all I could to block out the pain and started tensing up.

As we rose up into the dark, I could see the lights of the other casinos all around. The moon was out. The fresh air was breezing by on us. The people walking up and down the Las Vegas Strip were far below us.

I saw up ahead the tracks, leading us to do crazy turns, including inverted loops. I wanted to block out all of the pain and fear I knew was coming.

Then, at that moment, while still on the slow upward incline, I came to two realizations.

First, I realized there was no way off this ride until it was over. I couldn't just stop and get off. I couldn't obey every cell in my body that was screaming at me to get out. I'd have to sit there and go through it all.

Second, more powerfully, I realized I didn't have to "try" to endure. I didn't have to brace against what was coming. I didn't have to try to block whatever fear and sensations would occur.

I could instead choose to embrace the experience. I thought, let's make the best of it. Let's allow myself to experience the fear, emotions, and sensations of being thrown in all directions as if I were an observer. And do it with my eyes wide open.

The roller coaster car arrived at the top of the incline. After a brief pause, it sped into a downward trajectory, jerking sideways, high above the buildings below. Then the car went into a loop, and I was upside down briefly. I felt the pressure of acceleration on my body from different angles.

All the while, I embraced the experience. I saw what was going on within me - the thrill, the fears, without being associated with it. It was like I was an observer having a front-seat experience in what was going on within me and around me, without being attached to any of it.

Despite hanging upside down briefly, I felt a sense of peace as I embraced and observed the sensations. I didn't resist them, as was my initial instinct.

Eventually, we returned inside the casino and walked off the rollercoaster car. Once the ride was over, I felt profound gratitude for this experience and the last-minute realization that I could embrace rather than resist. I also appreciated my friend Morris for encouraging me to go on the ride.

Soon after, I moved out of Las Vegas. I didn't really think much more about this experience. It had been one of many pleasant experiences in building courage and facing my fears. But little did I know that within this experience laid the seeds of a tool that would help free me from hundreds of fears.

Blog Posting

A couple of years later, I wanted to set up a personal blog site. As part of learning to live from my heart, I wanted to express myself to the world. I wanted to share what I knew and had learned.

I had a bad experience many years earlier when I first went online. I had posted things on a Usenet group under my real name. I thought it would be private for that group. Later, when the internet became widely used, anything I had posted could instead be found by anyone. I felt haunted by it for many years. I was fearful of making the same mistake again. So, I would write posts on various forums but always under a pseudonym. I wouldn't use my real name.

But now, to live from the heart, I felt called to stop hiding my identity or who I was.

So, I set up my own personal blog site. I put my real name on top of it. I then sat on my computer and wrote a blog post. It wasn't controversial. It was relatively simple. I reviewed it probably 10 times to make sure it was ok. I liked it. I felt good about it. Then I hit the "post" button.

For a few minutes, I was happy. Then, I wondered what people might think of it. All of a sudden, it felt like a sledgehammer hit my body. My heart started beating faster, and my stomach tensed up. My thoughts were darting, *"This is a disaster!"*. The area in my torso became painful. I felt terrified about my post. I didn't know what to do; it was too painful.

I went to my computer, logged into the site, and deleted the post.

A wave of feel-good hormones hit my veins as soon as I did. My entire body relaxed. My breathing became normal. My heart rate subsided. The pain was gone. My body felt good again.

While my body felt good, mentally, I felt frustrated. That primal fear came up a lot for me! I wanted to do something. But my body would react in pain. Or it would freeze me. It would prevent me from doing what I wanted to do.

It would take a lot of effort and time to overcome my fears - as it did during the Free Hugs. With intense mental effort, I did progress over time. But at this rate, it would take several lifetimes for me to overcome all the fears I wanted to overcome. It was crazy.

Fear Experience Tool

One day, I received insights on overcoming this when listening to an audio program. In that program, I heard about a method to process emotions and triggers. It sounded weird. However, it was similar to the experience I had with the rollercoaster. I decided to test the tool on something the program hadn't discussed: panic-like fears. Specifically, posting a blog post under my real name.

Following the instructions, I sat in my chair at home and closed my eyes. I then imagined I had posted a blog post online under my real name. It felt real, and I felt my body experience the fears. My stomach felt pain, my heart rate increased, and my breathing became shallow. However, I simply observed what happened instead of panicking or fighting it. While my body was experiencing the fear as if I had done it, my mind knew I hadn't yet. Thus, I felt safe experiencing all of these sensations.

With my eyes closed, I watched its effects on my body. My role was simply to observe the effects. The shape it had. The color. The texture. I did not try to change anything. I was only observing.

Following the instructions, I also repeated to myself: "I am allowing myself to experience this fear of my post," over and over. This was to help me stay focused on simply experiencing and observing the fear rather than trying to change anything. As I observed the fear with my eyes closed, I noticed that the shape, texture, and color of the fear within me changed. It morphed into different shapes, textures, and colors. I didn't try to create any change. It seemed to change on its own as I observed it.

After about 20 minutes of sitting there and visualizing, the pain and fear stopped. It was an odd sensation. It was like the fear had just gotten up and left my body. I felt a sense of peace and completeness.

Then, following the instruction, I asked myself, "What is the lesson?". I wrote it down.

I then went to my computer and thought I'd try to post the blog post for real. I wanted to see what would happen. Would I feel massive fear and pain afterward and feel the compulsion to delete it?

I hit "publish" on the post, under my blog, with my real name. I waited a few minutes. I felt calm. Ten minutes later, I still felt relaxed. By now, I would typically be curling on my bed in pain. Instead, I felt no pain in my torso. My breathing was normal. My heart rate was standard. I was calm. I was awestruck.

I tried again a few days later to ensure it wasn't a fluke. I processed the fear with the tool before posting, then posted again, and I felt fine. It worked again.

I was blown away. A new world had opened for me.

So, I immediately started applying it repeatedly to so many fears. Fear of going out on a date? Applied it. Fear of doing country line dancing for the first time in front of people I knew? Applied it. Fear of going up in a hot air balloon? Applied it. Fear of my upcoming job interview for a dream job? Applied it. Fear of skydiving? Applied it. Over the following years, I used it hundreds of times.

It revolutionized my life. I no longer needed to be held back by crushing, deliberating fears. I felt a sense of liberation after using the tool for several years. I didn't have to be boxed in anymore. Anything anyone did, I could also eventually do. I had thought overcoming most of my fears would take me several lifetimes.

But now I knew it wouldn't. I could do it in this lifetime with time to spare.

My Reflection

I couldn't find an official name for the tool for many years. The audio program I learned it from didn't give it a name. So, I called it "The Fear Experience Tool," or FE for short.

Years later, as I was in the final stages of editing this book, I came across a similar tool with a few differences. That tool is called TAME from the book "Happiness Trap" by Russ Harris. I've found that tool to be very helpful and would recommend it.

I've guided others through this tool, which has proven impactful for them. Sometimes, it took a five-minute session to work through the fear. Sometimes it took a 90-minute session. I developed a personal rule that after 30 minutes, I would stop for the day and resume the next day. This tool requires much concentration, so I liked taking breaks between sessions.

I found that occasionally, I'd need to apply FE multiple times to the same situation. In those cases, that'd tell me that the underlying fear wasn't resolved, and I'd need to use a different tool and/or dig deeper. Nevertheless, if I wanted to take action, FE would help me greatly, regardless of the present fear.

I also found that after applying FE, I might still be slightly nervous about the situation. However, I discovered that nervousness to be manageable, unlike the crushing fear I'd experienced before using that tool.

Your Reflection

Have you ever had that experience of being willing to do something, but your body just won't cooperate?

What would you love to do that you are mentally okay with but that your body keeps you from doing out of a sense of terror?

Chapter 6

Planning for the Best,
Prepared for the Worst
The Story of Unemployment

As I started my last semester in graduate school, I faced a dilemma. What would I do after graduation? Work at a job I didn't have the heart to work in? Or face unemployment until I had a career aligned with living from the heart?

I had set myself on the path to graduate from business school before deciding to align with love. Once I chose to align with love, I was only a few months away from moving over 1,000 miles to start graduate school. My world had been thrown upside down. I didn't know what else to do. So, I continued the path of quitting my job at the oil company and going to graduate school. That seemed the best thing to do until I could figure out otherwise.

Now that I was getting close to graduating, I didn't like the jobs coming down the school's pipelines. Not after two years of working toward overcoming my fears and aligning with love.

If I became unemployed again, it wouldn't be my first time.

Unemployment, the First Time

Nine years earlier, I had graduated with my bachelor's degree in computer science. I also had a few years of experience working in the aerospace industry on a defense project.

I had selected computer science for my bachelor's degree because I was too afraid to pursue my desired degree: Business.

By the time graduation came around, I was also feeling queasy about my career path. I wanted my life to be about uplifting humanity, not creating weapons of war.

A few months before graduation, I went to a Tony Robbins workshop. While being pumped up during the workshop, I decided to walk away from it all. I felt powerful at the time. I was sure it'd only be a few months before I would succeed in a new career.

After the workshop, I stopped showing up for the scheduled job interviews. One of those employers called me after I was a no-show. They still wanted to interview me, but I declined.

Thus, I walked away from a secure, lucrative career upon graduation. I moved to Kentucky to stay with a friend. I then tried to get work in the space exploration field for a non-software position. I thought that would help humanity.

I failed to get hired. Within a few months, I ran out of money.

That's when I entered a world of hurt. I didn't expect to fail. Did I throw away my life?

I left Kentucky and drove around parts of the country while panicked. Ended up in Georgia. Moved in with another friend. Got a job at a bookstore to make money to eat and pay rent.

For the next few years, I worked at a series of places, such as Taco Bell, factories, and Walmart. All doing entry-level jobs at low wages just to try to survive while experiencing deep depression.

I eventually returned to the city of my alma mater in Huntsville, Alabama, to roommate with my close friend Steve. I then started working at Target. I stayed there for four years. When people from my school or my former workplace would come into the store, I'd hide so they wouldn't see how far I had "fallen." These were hard times that felt like they would never end.

Eventually, I began to rebuild myself. Eventually, I started taking a few business classes I had always wanted to take. Then, I started working for the headquarters of an oil company in Oklahoma. It had taken a long time, but I was finally back to working behind a computer and making a decent wage. I used my time at the oil company to pay off my debt, save money, and apply for graduate school.

However, the experience left me scarred. I felt crushed by having been unemployed. For years, I would do anything to avoid unemployment again. Even if it meant working low wages and doing things I hated.

Post Graduate School

Back to the present, I was now graduating with my master's in business. Finally, getting the degree I had always wanted. I'm facing a similar dilemma. I didn't like the jobs coming down the school's pipeline. My boss at the oil company had let me know he wanted me to come back and work in the company's finance department. I'd be guaranteed a high wage if I did that. But I didn't resonate with any of that. It wasn't the path with the heart.

Do I accept jobs that don't align me with living from the heart? Or do I go down this dark path of unemployment again, knowing how disastrous it ended the first time?

I valued being employed as it helped me care for myself and the people around me. I'd have a lovely home to live in, health insurance, savings for retirement, and maybe a house. I'd be respected, and people would think well of me. My family would love it.

On the other hand, if I became unemployed, I'd risk my well-being. I might become homeless, would have no health insurance, and put no money aside for retirement. My world would shrink a lot as well. I'd lose the respect of people, and my family would hate it.

However, if I started working at a job I didn't resonate with, I felt I'd betray that part of me that wanted to learn to live from the heart and face his fears. That part of me that was dedicated to making an impact in the world and living his values at work.

As I thought of all of this, it became clear to me: I no longer wanted to be the kind of man who took on jobs he didn't like and ended up hating them. I didn't want to be putting hateful energy into the world due to the fears I had about quitting. That would not be living from the heart or be aligned with love.

Instead, I wanted to transform myself into a man who could live from the heart with his career and life.

If that meant I'd have to risk unemployment for a while, then so be it. I was going to face that demon again. Even if that demon caused me to wake up in the middle of the night scared as hell.

Preparations

During the last semester of graduate school, I started to prepare myself psychologically for the path ahead. I didn't know how long or hard the journey would be. I just knew I hadn't prepared psychologically for the journey the first time I was unemployed. That had been disastrous.

To prepare psychologically, first, I created a worst-case scenario. That way, my subconscious could be assuaged and cared for regardless of what happened. I figured doing that would keep me from panicking like the first time. And that I'd know what to do if the worst-case scenario arose.

Thus, I opened a Microsoft Word document and created a table with three columns.

In the first column, I wrote, "What might happen if I don't take these jobs? What if I wait to work until I can find a heart-centered job?"

I wrote that the worst-case scenario is that I become unemployed, perhaps permanently, and homeless with no money. I might become a beach bum - homeless and living near the beach.

In the second column, I wrote: "What is the likelihood of this happening?"

If I didn't take a job immediately, the likelihood of unemployment would be high. So, the possibility of running out of money was also very high.

In the third column, I wrote, "How can I mitigate the effect of the worst-case scenario?". That way, I could be mentally, emotionally, and psychologically okay if the worst-case scenario does happen.

As I worked through this, I decided that after years of putting hate and fear into my jobs, I was no longer willing to do so. I wanted to learn to live from the heart, to make decisions out of love, not fear. If it meant becoming homeless and unemployed, I could accept that. If I couldn't put positive energy into the world through my jobs, at least I'd avoid putting negative energy into the world.

That realization helped me feel at peace with the prospect. I'd do my best to search for a heart-centered job. But if I was unsuccessful, I accepted I might have to live like a homeless bum. That was better than the alternative of putting more hate into the world.

Second, I started listening to guided meditations my friend Boniebelle recommended. While listening to the guided meditation, I got an internal ping to start using the affirmation, "Something good is going to happen." I was to use this affirmation whenever I'd find myself at a crossroads in which I didn't know what to do next or what was coming next. Instead of going into a full-on panic, I'd affirm that something good was going to happen, without knowing what that would be. Thus, instead of imagining the worst, I would look to see what good could come.

Year 1

After graduation, I flew to France to visit my father and other family members. My father paid for the trip and for my expenses while there. After a month of vacation, I returned to the US. I had a little money, so I drove from Las Vegas, where I had graduated, to the coast of California to stay with a friend for a week. My friend offered to have me stay there longer, but I didn't resonate with being in the area. So, I drove to Oklahoma and stopped at my mother's place for a couple months. I started searching online for jobs.

Then, I drove to Georgia to visit a friend. Then, I went to North Carolina to stay at my sister's place for a month while she was away. I continued searching for jobs online.

Whenever I didn't know what to do or what was coming next, I'd affirm, "Something good is going to happen."

A few months later, my father emailed me asking why I didn't have a job yet. He wrote, "Didn't you learn your lesson nine years ago? Why haven't you secured a job right away yet?"

Then he emailed me, "You probably didn't even get your degree! That must be why you can't get a job!".

A couple of months later, when I finally received my physical diploma, I emailed him a picture. As I was still unemployed, he emailed me, "You must be a lazy bum!".

After four to five months, my mother offered to have me stay with her in Oklahoma until I landed a job. I resisted at first. I didn't want to be in my 30s living at my mother's place. But I had minimal funds left, and I thought it'd help to have a stable base to look for a job. So, I accepted and started living at her place.

Once back in Oklahoma, my old boss at the oil company found out I was in town. He sent word that he wanted to hire me back. I could use my graduate degree to work in the finance department at the company's headquarters. They would be paying me significantly more than I've ever made.

I thought about it. I had by then been unemployed for a few months. I was almost out of money. I didn't have any good job prospects. I did like my former boss, and I did like the people at the company. They were nice to me. It would be nice to start earning a wage, saving money for retirement, building equity in a home, having health insurance, and living on my own again. I'd be respected, and life would be easier.

But if I went back to work there, by the nature of the organization, I'd have to hide who I was. I'd be inauthentic. I'd go back there out of fear, not love. I'd be betraying myself.

I declined.

I reaffirmed to myself that I'd rather be unemployed than end up putting hateful energy into the world again. "Something good is going to happen," I affirmed.

One day, while sitting at the desk and looking for jobs online, I realized this job search might take a long time. I set an intention that no matter how long I'd be unemployed, this period of life would help me become a much better employee than ever before. Rather than emerge from unemployment broken like I had been the first time, I was determined to emerge out of it much better this time. My future employer would benefit.

May 2011: I woke up one day near my birthday thinking, "I've now been unemployed for one full year." That felt heavy to me. A whole year unemployed. Far longer than my first time. My funds were gone. I'm still living with my mother. I'm still looking for a job I can do.

Year 2

My mother accepted a job in Dallas, Texas. She soon moved there. I stayed in Oklahoma for a month or two to fix the house to sell. Then, I moved to Dallas with her.

This new house was bigger than the old house. She asked if I could take 4-6 hours a week to clean it up. In return, she'd give me some pocket money. I agreed.

One day, my mother was frustrated with how long my job search was taking. She said I should just take any job that came up. I refused. I said, "The minute you decide you want me out of this house, no problem. Let me know, and I'll be out within 24 hours."

My mother never took me up on the offer. I think she was more afraid of me being homeless than I was.

I was looking for jobs I'd resonate with and applying to them online. I was emailing potential employers as well. No hit so far.

I also started attending a few local networking meetings for job seekers. It felt so incredibly awkward being there. I didn't know what to say or do at those meetings. After a while, I stopped going.

I sometimes walked outside, feeling hopeless about ever landing a job. Sometimes, I wondered if I had made a mistake when I gave up the lucrative jobs at the aerospace company and then the oil company to go on this path. Would I ever succeed?

I eventually found the answer to the question, "Who would ever date a grown unemployed man with no money who lives with his mom?"

The answer is: "Grown women who also live with their parents."

May of 2012: Near my birthday, I woke up thinking, "Two years now of being unemployed." Will I ever land a job?

Year 3

Since I didn't know anyone in Dallas, I joined a board gaming group to meet people and connect. I started volunteering there.

I battled feelings of hopelessness that I'd ever land a job. Sometimes, my moods would swing widely. It was impacting my ability to conduct a job search. I wasn't afraid of being homeless or unemployed, but I wanted to keep making progress in my job search. Feeling hopeless was making it so hard. I didn't want to give up.

I decided I needed to see a counselor. My mom offered to pay for it. After a series of psychological tests, the counselor said I was mildly depressed.

I replied, "No way! I'm not depressed. I've been depressed in the past. I know what it's like to be depressed. This isn't depression."

She nevertheless helped me work through the feelings of being unemployed. I started working through many of my emotional issues. With her encouragement, I also started mindful meditation.

As a result, I soon learned a lot about regulating my emotions. I underwent a lifestyle transformation once I learned to better manage my feelings. I started eating a lot healthier and exercising.

I continued reading self-improvement books, attending a few personal development workshops, and doing what I could to apply for jobs.

I also started volunteering for a spiritual center doing office work. That way, I could feel like I'm contributing in some way. I got to see how heart-centered the people at the spiritual center were and how they each worked to improve the lives of others. I thought about how much I'd love to work for a place like this one day. It felt much better than a corporate environment's cold and sometimes cutthroat nature.

Then, I joined a Toastmasters club and became club president. I also began providing pet care services for a friend and made a little money that way.

After reading Jack Canfield's book "The Success Principles," I put up things on my walls to remind me of my past success. Diplomas, certificates, medals, and things I had achieved went up on my wall. That helped remind me that I wasn't a loser despite my situation. I was indeed capable of success.

One day, I finally had an interview! I applied for a job at the spiritual center where I had been volunteering. It was my first interview since graduation. I knew the woman who would be interviewing me. After the interview, I didn't hear anything back. A week later, I asked them about it. They said they had gone with someone else.

My father invited me to visit him in France. He would pay for everything. I missed France, and I knew I'd enjoy seeing him. However, I could imagine the conflicts if I went there unemployed. After all, he believed I was a lazy bum for being unemployed. I decided not to take him up on it. I decided that I would hold off on visiting France until I could be the one to finance my flight.

Around the same time, I decided I would not travel outside Dallas until I landed my job. I was digging in and didn't want to be distracted anymore.

I kept on trying to find jobs. Wondering if I'd ever land. Sometimes, in moments of weakness, I'd wonder if I made the right choice going down this path. Regardless, I was on this path and committed to seeing it through.

May 2013: One morning close to my birthday, I woke up with the distressing thought, *"I've now spent three years unemployed."*

I recently read that people who have been unemployed for more than one year are considered "chronically unemployed." The paper said they will most likely never be employed long-term again. I had been jobless so far for three years. I decided that that statistics would never apply to me. And that I'd do everything to ensure it wouldn't.

Year 4

A friend from Las Vegas contacted me, asking me to work part-time for her. I gladly accepted as she is heart-centered. I loved the work she did. I worked a few months remotely for about ten hours a week to help her publish a book. Though it wasn't full-time employment, I enjoyed the work. It helped me feel productive, too.

Soon after, I entered my first 5K running race to improve my fitness.

I started taking a 12-week workshop series on how to land a job. The series covered all aspects of a job search, from networking effectively to preparing a resume to interviewing.

As I went through the workshops, I realized I was going about my job search in a very fuzzy, unclear, and ineffective manner. What was the value I was bringing? What was I trying to create for the organization? What direction did I want to go?

My birthday was coming up soon. Instead of a physical gift, I asked my mother for the funds to hire a career coach. She agreed.

May 2014: On the morning of my birthday, I realized, "I've now been unemployed for four years." That felt heavy.

Year 5

I started meeting with my new career coach. She took an inventory of my job skills, volunteer and work history, and desires. She then said, "You should consider working for non-profit organizations."

I said, "What? No way! I have a business degree, and I like making profits. What's the point of working for an organization that doesn't make a profit?"

She said, "It fits everything you're looking for—the kind of people you want to work for, the kind of impact you want to make, and the kind of mission you have."

With her encouragement, I started networking with non-profit organizations. I took classes in non-profit management. I carried out informational interviews with over a dozen people who worked for non-profit organizations.

I liked what I heard, what I saw, and what I felt. I tailored my job search in that direction. I figured I could be a volunteer coordinator since I loved starting and leading as president of small volunteer organizations.

I also started working on my buttons or triggers. I began to expand my support network by joining a circle of men who met to help each other grow. I also started attending a spiritual center regularly on Sundays. I had now also joined two racing clubs and was running races regularly.

Near the end of year five, my mother was laid off. She had substantial savings, but I didn't want to deplete her resources.

"Mom, If I don't have a job by the end of December, I'm moving out," I said. I'd sleep in my car or couch surf if I needed to. It didn't matter.

She tried to persuade me that it was okay for me to stay with her. I said "no;" if I hadn't landed a job by the end of the year, I wanted to shake things up. I wasn't hopeless but frustrated and didn't want to do the same thing forever if it wasn't working.

May of 2015: A few days before my birthday, I woke up concerned that I had been unemployed for five years.

Year 6

I told my counselor on one of my now rare visits to see her: "You told me three years ago that you thought I was mildly depressed. I refused to accept it at the time. I said you were wrong."

I continued, "However, I see now that you were right. I'm experiencing such a level of well-being and joy regularly now. I've never experienced that before. I can now see how I was mildly depressed back then."

I had spent so many years being deeply depressed that being only mildly depressed seemed like a significant improvement. It didn't feel like depression to me. Only when I started to experience living with regular joyfulness and happiness could I tell the difference.

Despite the stress of the upcoming deadline to find a job or move out, I was enjoying my life. I had dealt with and shed so much emotional and mental baggage over the last few years. I also jettisoned a lot of unhealthy habits. I created powerful practices, such as no longer eating junk food, starting to exercise regularly, and meditating in the morning. I had been building a healthy network of friends among different interest communities in Dallas. I was living more from the heart than ever before.

Thanks to what I learned in the 12-week job searching workshops, I pursued non-profit job opportunities by networking and talking with people. I attended networking meetings every week and met with other job searchers regularly. As a result of the feedback I received through my networking meetings, I changed the job I was targeting. Instead of targeting a volunteering coordinator job, I'd target a non-profit financial job. That aligned more with my job experience and education. Plus, it suited my personality better.

I also continued working part-time for my friend from Las Vegas, though my work now only took about 20 minutes a month.

Finally, I found a job I was so excited to apply for.

It was a full-time job as the financial operation manager at a spiritual center. In early December, they set up an interview for me in early January.

This meant that I had a month to prepare for the interview. I stopped all other job search activities and concentrated entirely on this one. Every day, I went to the library to study and prepare. I hadn't done accounting since graduate school, so I started rereading accounting books.

On the way to the library every day, I'd listen to Eminem's song "Lose Yourself." This was my one shot at this fantastic job opportunity. The only day I took off was Christmas Day.

I also spent countless hours preparing a spreadsheet of all the possible questions I could be asked during the interview. Then, I wrote all the possible answers I could give. I paid particular attention to the questions I feared the most because, as I learned in the workshop, that's the question they are most likely to ask me.

The question I feared the most was, "What is your experience with QuickBooks?". The job required "Proficiency" in QuickBooks. I had never used the software. So, I took a class that month on QuickBooks and read several books on it. I formulated an answer showcasing my history of rapidly learning software in different industries, plus the active steps I was now taking to learn QuickBooks.

Then, I started practicing the interviews with my mom. She filled in the role of the hiring manager, asking me questions. First, we practiced many times in my regular clothes. Then, I started wearing my business suit for the practice interviews. I wanted to make the practice as authentic as possible.

Never in my life had I wanted a job as much as this one. Never in my life had I ever prepared as much for an interview as I had for this one. I did everything I could to ensure I gave it my best shot.

Finally, the day of the interview came. I was interviewed by the two executive ministers. They invited me to come back for a technical interview with a subject expert. After that, I was asked to come back to conduct an interview with the peers I'd be working with.

After the staff interview, I was offered the full-time position. I accepted with so much joy and gratitude.

My journey from being unemployed to landing my dream job had been successful. A new journey had now started.

Postscript

I had told my mom I would move out by the end of December if I hadn't landed a job by then. However, since I had an interview in early January, I delayed moving out until the interview process ended. She was happy to keep me there longer.

After getting hired and working full-time, I stayed at my mom's place a few months longer as I prepared to move out. However, I happily started paying her rent. Finally, after being at my job for five months, I moved out to my own place. I was finally living on my own for the first time in a long time. While I was grateful to have lived at my mom's place, it was nice to be king of my place again.

The first year at my new full-time job was tough. The phrase from the Peace Corps, "The toughest job you'll ever love," came to mind so much to describe my first year. I had much to learn about the non-profit industry, spiritual center operations, my job as the accounting manager and donor relation person, and working so inter-connectedly with others in a small office.

In my first year, the center was simultaneously experiencing a capital campaign and building expansion. There was so much going on. The learning curve was steep, and it stayed steep during that first year. I wanted to do everything I could to make sure I was successful.

About one year after I had started working, on a Sunday, I was sitting in the back of the sanctuary during the spiritual service. About two hundred people were in attendance. The minister I reported to was speaking from the podium at the front of the sanctuary. At the end of the service, she announced to everyone that I had worked there for an entire year. She lauded how I had made a big difference for the organization during my time there.

After those words, I saw everyone stand up, turn around to face me, and applaud me joyfully. As I looked around at everyone celebrating me, I felt a wave of emotion wash over me.

I had made it. I had succeeded in my new job.

A couple years later, I flew to visit my father in France. I financed the flight myself.

Eight years later, as I edited this chapter, I was still working full-time for non-profit organizations that make a difference in the world. While I no longer worked full-time for the first non-profit organization that hired me, I've remained fully employed for the entire eight years.

That statistic said that people who were unemployed for over a year would be "chronically unemployed" and wouldn't be able to keep working long term afterward? That didn't apply to me. As I had decided it wouldn't.

My Reflection

I lost a lot in those years of unemployment—the income, the addition to my retirement account, the payments toward having my own house, and the skillsets I could have learned on the job. I also didn't travel out of town for years despite my love of travel. I didn't date much after the first couple of years. I also caused a lot of worry for my family as well.

But I gained so much—I was able to face a terrible fear and come out much better. I shed so much emotional, physical, and mental baggage. I also learned to be more connected to myself and my local communities. I finally started a long-term habit of eating healthy and running. Those days of unemployment helped me become so much more the man I wanted to be—a man so much more heart-centered and courageous than he ever had been before.

Could I have done all that by staying employed at the oil company or elsewhere? Maybe. I don't know. Maybe other people could have. But in my case, I don't think so. I'd likely have been stuck being comfortable making a higher wage and not wanting to rock the boat. I may not have taken the risks to grow in the way I was able to grow.

In retrospect, I was also fortunate to have a mother who could provide a place to stay and give me food to eat. I hadn't planned on that. I also didn't plan on being unemployed for so long. I'm also lucky I didn't have any health issues, given my lack of health insurance.

Before becoming unemployed, I had spent a long period of introspection. I decided to trust that I would be guided, that something good would happen and that my principles and decision to follow the course of my heart would work out. I'm glad it worked out for me.

Here are some of the tools that helped me deal with the fears:

- Worst-Case Scenario Analysis. Listing out the worst-case scenario and how I could mitigate it or be at peace helped turn what could have been a situation where I panicked into a situation where I'd stay calm. Sure, I did feel hopeless sometimes that I'd ever succeed in landing a job. But I never felt profoundly depressed or panicked. That's a significant difference from the first time I was unemployed.
- Affirming "Something good is going to happen" whenever I was at a crossroads or unsure what would come up. I affirmed that countless times. It also helped me stay calm in the face of uncertainty.
- Setting a powerful intention that regardless of how long my unemployment period lasted, I would emerge a much better employee for it. That helped me continue to focus on my growth.

Your Reflection

What is the biggest fear you've ever faced and overcome? What tools, mindsets, and practices helped you overcome the fear?

What is a considerable fear you've been avoiding dealing with that you'd love to face and overcome one day?

What tools and mindsets can you use to face that fear?

What could be on the other side of that fear once you've successfully faced it?

Building Habits

"Forget Inspiration. Habit is more dependable. Habit will sustain you whether you're inspired or not."

Octavia Butler

Chapter 7

Building Willpower
The Story of the Promise Book

A couple years before the Green Wig event, when I was around 28 or 29, I woke up one morning. I was in that twilight state before becoming fully conscious of who I was or where I was. At that moment, a thought came to my awareness, *"This isn't who you really are."*

Meaning: I was not the person I was living as. I was more than that. My current life wasn't reflective of who I was.

Then, a tidal wave of reality came crashing into my consciousness. I was deeply depressed, working a dead-end job for little money. I felt like a total loser and socially disconnected. I had almost no social life. I mindlessly played a lot of computer games and binged junk food to numb the massive pain I was experiencing.

I didn't know what to do about the thought. I moved on with my day. Got ready for work.

Later, a week or two later, I'd wake up with that same thought. It happened every so often.

Breaking the promise

Meanwhile, on a separate front, I was scheduled to meet my friend Zorine on my day off. We had been good friends for about eight years.

That day, I didn't feel like meeting with her. I didn't feel like following up with our plans. There was no specific reason for the change. It often happened that I'd set out to do something and then decided not to do it.

I emailed her: "I'd like to postpone our meeting to another time."

She wrote back immediately. "OK, but I don't want to set up a meeting with you again. I look so forward to meeting with you, and you've canceled many times. I feel sad and disappointed each time. I don't want to go through this disappointment again."

I was stunned.

Had I sunk so low that my dear friend couldn't rely on me? This was my treasured friend, whom I had spent so much time with while in college. It hurt that my friend couldn't depend on me to attend a simple get-together. I also realized it reflected how I was showing up in all parts of my life.

After reading Zorine's email, I decided I didn't want to live like that. I didn't want to be that kind of person. So, I decided to do something about it. What could I do about that? How could I become more reliable? How could I follow through with my plans with Zorine and other areas of my life?

The Promise Book

I bought a small notebook that fits in the pockets of my pants. I placed a pen along with it. I wrote on the first page, "Promise Book." I set myself a challenge: make and keep 100 promises to myself. At least one promise a day. Each time I made a promise, I'd write it down in the notebook. I'd then check it off when I had kept my promise. I'd try to have only one outstanding commitment at a time.

I didn't tell anyone else I was doing this. If I accomplished all 100 promises, I decided to buy myself a nice pin I wanted as a reward. I wanted to build mental muscle to keep my promises. I had read that making promises was like working out. The more we practice making and keeping promises, the more we strengthen our promise-keeping "muscles."

My first promise: "Put the laundry in the washing machine today." That would be a significant achievement if I kept the promise.

Later that day, I put the laundry in. I felt relieved that I met my written promise. It wasn't easy.

I set another promise the next day: "Take the trash out." My roommate had been on me for not doing that promptly. I took out the trash that day. I felt a sense of achievement. Baby steps, but I must start where I am.

After ten days, I had kept ten promises. I started to feel refreshed and a little more confident in myself. I kept doing it. Every day, I wrote down one thing I had promised myself I would do. I started having fun with it. I liked building a habit of keeping my promises.

Within a few months, I had kept all 100 promises. I felt a sense of accomplishment reaching that. I felt a little lighter. I could start to trust myself again and honor my commitments. I never did buy that pin for myself. So I wasn't perfect. However, I saw that keeping my promises was fun.

This wasn't the one-and-be-all of becoming disciplined and building habits. However, it was a start. An important start. It changed my life.

I stopped canceling meetings with my friends because of being "lazy." While I've had to back out of meetings due to unanticipated conflicts, no friend has ever told me again that they didn't want to set up an appointment because they were fearful I wouldn't follow through.

As I continued to grow and follow up on my commitments, I worked through massive problems in my life. That led to changing my view of myself. It also led to building foundational habits that empowered me. Habits that would eventually lead me to learn how to live more from the heart.

Eventually, I stopped waking up with the thought, *"This isn't who you are."*. I had started living much more aligned with who I really was.

My Reflection

What did building discipline and creating habits have to do with learning to live from the heart? It helped create a more solid foundation for living life. If living from the heart is like building a house, then creating habits and improving discipline is like making a solid foundation for the home.

Many years later, people would occasionally comment on how disciplined I was. As if it was a "natural-born" trait of mine. As if I had been like that all along. And write off what I do as something unreachable for them because they don't have the trait of being disciplined.

My instinctual response for a long time was, "*No, I'm not a naturally disciplined person.*" Whatever discipline and good habits I have, I had to build up from scratch using psychological tools. And if I can build it from scratch, others can also build it from whatever level they start.

It was only much later, while writing this book, that I decided to stop resisting this label. Yes, I'm a disciplined person. I wasn't. But now I am.

The promise book was an essential step toward that.

Your Reflection

On a level of 1 to 10, how do you rank yourself on keeping your agreements and commitments to yourself and others?

How do you feel about your response?

Chapter 8

Changing Habits
The Story of Coca-Cola

In 2007, the year before the Green Wig events, I started working at the headquarters of an oil company in Oklahoma. One of the perks of working there was access to unlimited free soda drinks for any employee. That included Coca-Cola, my soda of choice. It wasn't far either, as the fridge was beside my office.

At first, it felt like heaven. *"Oh my god,"* I thought, *"as many cokes as I want, and I don't have to pay for it?"* That was such a fantastic concept. I adored it.

For years, I had been drinking only one or two cokes a day. I had thought at different times of quitting it. I was concerned about how unhealthy it was to drink sugared water every day. I had read about the corrosive effects cokes had on the body. But I hadn't stopped drinking it. It was too irresistible.

Now that I had unlimited access to Coca-Cola on weekdays, I started drinking it much more. I eventually settled into drinking about six cokes a day. Not the diet or caffeine-free variety. I didn't care about those. Instead, I drank the fully caffeinated sugared Coca-Cola.

Soon, I started to feel the effects of drinking so much every day. I felt bloated. I also felt like my veins were full of artificial liquids. Then, I started needing to drink a Coke to wake up in the morning. I felt tired and irritable if I missed my regular Coke with its caffeine during the day. It also took a long time to fall asleep at night. Regardless, I had to have it.

30-Day Habit Trials

Alongside this development, I also experimented with 30-day habit trials. I learned the concept from personal development blogs I had been reading. The idea was to commit to changing a habit for only 30 days rather than committing to it for a lifetime.

Psychologically, setting out to change a habit for only 30 days is more manageable. Initially, committing to a new habit for a lifetime makes it more daunting and more likely to fail. The hardest part of changing a habit is in the first 30 days. Deciding to keep the habit after 30 days if we choose to do so is much easier.

Plus, we don't know if the benefits we imagine the new habit will give us will actually come to fruition. How can we know if we haven't done it yet? However, after 30 days, we usually experience some of the benefits of the new habit. We can then make a better decision on whether to continue in the long term.

I was curious if I could apply the 30-day habit trial framework to my addiction to drinking cokes.

I also wanted to see how healthier I'd be without drinking any cokes. I wanted to feel more natural. I also wanted to rely on natural energy sources rather than artificial sources.

First Attempt

On June 18 of that year, I launched a 30-day trial of not drinking a single Coca-Cola.

A habit isn't changed in a vacuum. A new habit needs to replace a bad habit. Thus, I decided to replace drinking Coke and consuming caffeine with water and juices.

After 30 days, I could decide whether to abstain or return to drinking Coke.

I made it through the first day. Victory! One full day without cokes or caffeine.

On the second day, failure! I had such an intense craving for drinking cokes. I gave in and drank one.

My 30-habit trial had lasted all of one day. The addiction felt so intense. I couldn't make it through the second day.

That night, I wrote in my journal:

> *"Result - 1st day great, 2nd day, cracked and stayed off this plan. I missed the staying-up power and the satisfaction of drinking Coca-Cola due to filling my stomach and the physiology change. When I'm feeling disempowered/mad/ upset/moody, I want to drink it. So, I know this lightweight approach will not work. I need to choose another approach."*

I was also trying a new psychological way of seeing failure. The next day, I wrote in my journal:

> *"If I fail...it does not reflect the inner me. It is simply a reflection that the method itself did not work well.... (This*

means) I could work on changing the method. Like I am going to do with the Coke Abstinence (30-Day Habit Trial). Previously, if I failed at something, it meant that I was not fixed up, that something was still wrong with me. Since I was trying to fix what was wrong with me, and if a method failed, then I was still wrong. Obviously, that put me under a huge strain of negativity and disempowering identity. My identity was tied to succeeding. That's not the right way to go about it. I like the new way better."

That new way of seeing success and failures helped me keep from beating myself up. I'd just need to figure out another method to make this successful. I returned to drinking as many Coca-Colas as I wanted to. I did notice that I wasn't entirely drinking the six cans a day I had been drinking before. Sometimes, I'd drink less.

Second Attempt

A few months later, on September 29, I started the 30-day trial of not drinking cokes again. I wanted to try again and see if I could be successful this time. I had recently succeeded in other 30-day habit trials, which gave me some confidence. I also gained an idea for raising my chance of success.

At the end of the first day, I wrote a "1" on the whiteboard in my fridge. My goal was to make it to "30." I thought writing it on the board would motivate me and make me more likely to succeed.

After completing the second day, I removed "1" and wrote "2" on the whiteboard. I felt a sense of achievement. It was like a reward to get to update the number. I looked forward to the end of each day to update the count. I continued updating the numbers as 2 became a 3 until I had written the number 6 on the fridge. I was fortunate to not experience any of the headaches that other people get when they stop consuming caffeine.

However, by Day 7, I felt tired and weak. I had gone a week without caffeine, Coke, or other sodas. I felt such an overwhelming craving. The siren song of Coca-Cola seductively called out to me. I couldn't hold out anymore. I gave in.

I went back to drinking cokes as much as I felt called to. I noticed I didn't drink as much as before, though I still drank too much.

A few months later, I was driving across Oklahoma while listening to a motivational audio program from Zig Ziglar. I started feeling intense disgust at my addiction to caffeinated drinks. I felt like I was a slave to this desire. I didn't feel free to walk away.

Freedom is my most important value, yet here I was, unable to stop this habit.

I started to feel such an intense determination to do something about it. At that moment, while driving in the countryside, I decided to do everything it took to remove the shackles that bound me to this godforsaken habit!

While driving, I reviewed my previous failures to stop drinking Coca-Cola. I analyzed why I failed. I figured I would counter each weak point. I wasn't going to rely on willpower alone. I had built up my will and discipline, but it wasn't enough. So, I created an entirely new plan of attack, specifically designed to tackle the weak points of my previous attempts.

I briefly considered a strategy of slowly drinking less and less each week. While that may work for some, I knew from experience that it wouldn't work for me. Instead, I needed to stop cold and put all my energy into it.

The next day, I wrote in my journal:

> *"Why: To be a free man. Up to me to be a free man, not up to anyone else. If I am to claim freedom for myself, I have to free myself first from my own vices, and then I can take freedom for me from others who seek to restrict me."*

This was way more powerful than just doing it for health reasons. My most important value is freedom. Associating this habit change with freedom would give me more oomph to my energy and willpower. It'd be like adding turbo fuel to a rocket ship. While willpower wasn't enough to make this habit change successful, I still needed as much willpower as possible during the initial stages.

Then, once I stopped driving, I took out my journal and listed 18 possible tactics I could engage in during this 30-day trial.

Some of them were:

> *"- No pasta at night, only veggie and meat.*
> *- Eat healthy lunches, nothing heavy, just light.*
> *- Walk (up and down the stairs) every 2 hours for 10 minutes."*
> *- Exercise vigorously for at least 30 minutes daily - walk fast, or aerobic or muscular - to the point of sweating and having a good workout.*
> *- Drink a lot of water during the day."*

This was to deal with the fatigue that came with caffeine withdrawal.

The part about drinking water was tricky. Unlimited sodas were available in the fridge, but there were no water bottles.

To deal with that, I bought several cases of 24-pack water bottles. Then, I brought them over to my workplace on the weekend. I put them in the elevators and brought them to the sixth floor, where my office was. Then, I took the cases one by one to my office. I wanted it to be easier to reach for water than for soda.

I also wrote other tactics and strategies in my journal. Some of which I followed and some I didn't.

One thing I did decide to try was to avoid eating Snickers bars during the trial. Every time I ate a candy bar, I felt a compulsion to drink a Coke. It was like a Pavlov association. I decided to refrain from eating candy bars for 30 days to avoid being tempted to drink cokes.

Finally, I wrote in my journal:

> *"My health is more important than anything else - more than work, more than anything, period. My body is my only temple for this time around."*

For 30 days, I decided nothing was more important than succeeding in this trial. Not my job. Not my finances. Not my application to graduate school. Nothing else mattered as much as this. I didn't want to sabotage myself again by using the excuse that I needed to be energetic for my job.

However, I wanted to keep my job and keep working on my application for graduate school. With this new mindset, the question no longer became, "What if I'm too tired to perform at work?"

Instead, the question became, "How can I ensure I have the energy to perform at work while being committed to my 30-day trial of no caffeine?"

Third Attempt

One day later, on November 26, I launched my third attempt.

I woke up that morning, visualizing success. I went outside in the dark to walk vigorously for 30 minutes. It was cold, but I wanted to ensure I exercised before going to work to help with my energy. I took a shower and visualized feeling successful after going without Coke for 30 days.

Two hours into work, I took my scheduled 15-minute break to walk up and down the stairs of the 12-story building. I felt re-energized and awake when I returned to my office.

I closed the door to my office for the first time during my lunch hour. Then, I rolled out a yoga mat. I laid down on it and set the timer for 45 minutes. I closed my eyes for a restful nap. I didn't fall asleep, but I did go into that twilight zone between being fully asleep and fully awake. When the alarm rang, I woke up refreshed. I then ate a light, microwavable lunch at my desk. Finally, once my lunch hour ended, I opened my door and returned to work.

Two hours after lunch, I again walked up and down the stairs for 15 minutes. I came back energized.

That evening, I wrote a "1" on the whiteboard on the fridge at home. I felt a sense of accomplishment. Then I went to sleep early.

Each weekday, I continued the same routine. Morning vigorous walk. At 10 a.m., walk up and down the stairs for 15 minutes. At lunchtime, I'd close my door, nap, and then eat a light lunch. At 3pm, I'd return to walking up and down the stairs for 15 minutes. Weekday evening meals, no heavy pasta. I drank a lot of water. All that was to ensure I had the energy to go through massive caffeine withdrawal.

On the eighth day, I wrote in my journal:

> *"I feel so much better physically, very little to no tiredness. I feel so good. I'm able to think much clearer; it's not as fuzzy... I'm able to move better and walk around better. My mind is becoming "tougher"...*
> *...However, the work is not over; the vigilance is not done. I still have to pay close attention to my body and emotions to make sure I manage this through."*

On December 25, I celebrated 30 days of being free from caffeine and soda. I had moved heaven and earth to make it happen. It was the sweetest Christmas gift I received that year. I felt so joyous and such a sense of freedom.

I also managed to keep my job.

For the next few months, I craved drinking Coca-Cola at least once daily. It was now easy to ignore. It didn't take willpower anymore, as I was now used to ignoring that craving.

The cravings eventually started to come only once a week. Then once a month. Then, once a year for a few years. And finally, it stopped altogether.

I noticed I had an easier time waking up and falling asleep. My body felt cleaner and more natural. In addition, I learned to listen to my body about the need for sleep and rest. For example, a year later, I went to graduate school. While my classmates were staying up late at night studying and drinking caffeine to do so, I'd instead go to bed early. Then, I'd wake up early in the morning to study.

Overall, I loved my new habit. Fifteen years later, I still had not drunk any soda or consumed any caffeinated drinks.

My Reflection

Changing my habit of drinking Coca-Cola and caffeine helped my body feel more natural and aligned me more with how I wanted to live. However, I didn't think giving up caffeine or sodas was necessary to live from the heart (even though, in my case, it helped). More powerfully, this trial gave me insights into using the 30-day framework to make far-reaching changes in my life.

That's not to say that willpower and discipline weren't necessary. They were essential to launch the habit. They were like the fuel to the rocket ship that goes up into space. Most of the energy from launching a rocket into space would be used in the first few minutes to get to orbit. Then, very little energy would be used to keep it going beyond Earth. For a habit, most of the energy in setting it up was used in the first few weeks.

However, I found that discipline and willpower weren't enough to make a habit stick long-term (or even just 30 days, as was in this case with Coca-Cola's case). I needed something I call "self-sufficiency"—that is, my new habit had to replace the need that the "bad" or "unhealthy" habit gave me.

All bad habits meet at least one need, even if the habit is harmful and hurts other needs. Thus, what finally helped me change the Coca-Cola habit was identifying what caffeine gave me (energy) and finding an alternative way to meet that need.

I've since tried the 30-day framework for changing or installing habits many times. I haven't always been successful. However, the times I was successful were when I found better alternatives to meet the core need that the unhealthy habit met.

Slowly, with this framework, I started to install many habits that created a more robust foundation for living from the heart. These habits included meditation, exercising, morning gratitude practice, etc.

To recap, some of the tools I used to replace the Coca-Cola habit:

- Committed to only 30 days before deciding whether to commit long-term. This reduced the psychological pressure of making the habit last. Only after 30 days, when it's easier to make a permanent decision, would I decide whether to stick to it long-term.
- Found an alternative habit that met the core need of the unhealthy habit.
- Connected the habit change with my most important value. That helped give more willpower during the first stage of launching the new habit.
- Looked ahead (or back) and found the potential failure points of installing a new habit. Then, I identified ways to address those potential failure points successfully.

- Saw failure not as a reflection of me but as a reflection of my method. Thus, if I failed, I tried again but changed some aspects of how I did it.

Your Reflection

If you could magically change one habit, what would it be?

These questions may help you to change an unhealthy habit:

- What needs, psychological or otherwise, do your bad habits meet?
- What is a healthier habit that could meet those needs?
- What significant value can you tie into your new habit so that you feel more intrinsically motivated to start the new habit?
- What failure points might you encounter when installing that new habit?
- How can you address those failure points so that if they arise, you can address the situation and still successfully install the new habit?

Chapter 9

Making Giant Changes
The Story of the Total Lifestyle Change

One evening in November 2012, I home cooked a pepperoni and cheese pizza with pineapples and anchovies. After I ate the delicious pizza, I ate some chocolate mint ice cream. I had stopped drinking sodas and caffeine five years earlier, but I hadn't stopped eating unhealthy foods.

The following day, I drove to the doctor for my first checkup in many years. I felt fearful I had developed diabetes. I needed chocolate in the morning to function. I felt old, sluggish, and slow despite only being in my mid 30's.

As I parked at the parking lot of the doctor's office, I felt scared. I didn't want confirmation that I had screwed up my health. I had been eating so much junk food over the last few years. It seemed that I might have developed diabetes as a result. I calmed myself down by reminding myself that knowing the truth is important. It would be better to know the truth than stay uncertain. Better to find out than to pretend everything was ok. I walked with trepidation into the doctor's office.

A week later, the nurse called with the results. She said, "Good news: You don't have diabetes. Bad news: your cholesterol levels are too high. Your triglyceride level needs to be at 149 or below, and it is currently at the dangerous level of 316." She also rattled off a lot of other bad cholesterol numbers.

Finally, she said, "If you don't change your lifestyle and lower it within 90 days, we need to put you on medication."

I felt relief. I had dodged a bullet. I hadn't yet developed diabetes due to my poor eating habits.

After feeling scared that I had screwed up my health by what I chose to eat, I felt like I had a second chance at being healthy. I wanted to make the most of my second chance.

It was concerning to me that my levels of cholesterol were so bad that I'd need to take medication. Those levels were primarily due to how I ate (with the lack of exercise playing a role). Thus, if I didn't change anything, I'd need to take medication due to what I chose to put in my mouth. That seemed crazy. In essence, if I continued eating the way I ate, I'd need to take pills to keep me alive.

I also yearned to travel around the world, especially to Asia. I wanted the freedom of being healthy enough to hike around the world. Eating so unhealthily that I would have to take cholesterol-lowering medication would cut back on my dreams of freedom. What if I was in some remote part of the world and lost my pills? Would my life be in danger? Seemed like I'd become a slave to those pills.

I immediately spent the afternoon researching how to improve my cholesterol numbers. I focused primarily on triglycerides, as that was my worst number. For my best chance of success, I would need to eliminate all the food I regularly ate, like ice cream, cheese, pasta, pizza, hot pockets, cakes, cookies, sweets, french fries, fried food, junk food, and almost all processed carbs.

I would instead need to eat healthy foods like vegetables, greens, legumes, nuts, fruits, baked chicken, and fish. I wasn't eating much of those at the time.

I also needed to go from being sedentary to walking at least 30 minutes daily.

I set out to lower my triglycerides from 316 to 149 in 90 days. That way, I'd be in the safe zone. Some authoritative websites said that was not possible in such a short timeline. But I was going to try anyway.

That day, I wrote in my journal:

> "I need to live medicine free. I don't want medicine in order to live. It will impede my East Asia trip and make me like Gene [Former multi-millionaire boss who ate a poor diet and died in his 50's, likely due to complications from his poor diet.] ... and all the old people at [former employment place]. I feel motivated and determined to do what it takes to lower cholesterol in 12 weeks."

First Attempt

I felt such a sense of urgency about getting started immediately. That afternoon, I went to a Subway restaurant. I ordered my first 100% vegetable sandwich with no cheese. As part of my new lifestyle, I decided to cut back on bread as it's a processed carb. The only occasion I'd allow myself to eat bread was for sandwiches that were 100% vegetable. It felt odd to eat that sandwich without the usual cheese or meat.

For the first few days, the new eating habit went well. I ate baked chicken, vegetables, fruits, and a combination of nuts and dried fruits for a snack.

On the evening of the second day, I wrote in my journal:

"I'm a poop making machine. I've pooped more often today than I can ever remember pooping in a day. Something like 5-6 times...

I feel like I'm coming out of a fog - a mental fog as well. A physical fog too.... I can think clearer. I can move clearer. I have a lot more energy. It's hard to believe that this is only day 2...!

Was I eating so much...processed stuff that it was shutting me down so much? ... and why it's shitting like crazy today now that [the body] has a break?

It's really extra-ordinary how much of a fog I feel has lifted up from me - I feel like my old self. A few days ago I remember thinking how I was so drugged down unlike before when I was younger and so energetic."

After a few days, I started to have cravings for all kinds of junk foods. But I stayed strong and kept going with my new eating style.

Later that day, I wrote in my journal:

"This is the most important thing for the next 90 days. Nothing else is more important than my health freedom....this takes absolute top priority in my decision-making.

This is part of loving myself tremendously. It's about loving my body. About loving myself enough that I will do what it takes to make sure that my [body] vehicle in this life is in proper order. It's about loving myself so much that I will move mountains."

Five days in, I craved ice cream. I missed feeling the cold texture of the ice cream on my tongue. I missed tasting these delightful, sweet flavors.

On day six, I couldn't resist that craving for ice cream anymore. I went to the fridge, opened a box of ice cream, and binged on it. That ended my first attempt.

Preparation Phase

Ok, I lasted only about six days on my first attempt. However, I reminded myself that changing my caffeine addiction had taken three attempts. Additionally, this new lifestyle change would be an order of magnitude more challenging than the Coca-Cola change.

For the next 12 days, I let myself eat junk food. I also carried on an intense research and planning phase on how to start again and, this time, succeed.

First, I knew I needed to deal effectively with emotional eating. I was addicted to junk food because it helped me bury my emotions. By burying them, I wouldn't have to deal with them.

Six months earlier, I had started reading the book "The Happiness Trap" by Russ Harris. I had only read half of it but learned some powerful tools. One such tool was diffusion, which could help process negative emotions. The tool, in a nutshell, is about remaining still and examining the thoughts coming into my mind. Reviewing these thoughts, especially after a triggering event, made me conscious and detached from them. I could then deal much more effectively with them and their resulting emotions.

The first time I tried it was after a first date. I felt icky after that date. I felt like eating so much junk food. When I applied the tool diffusion to see what thoughts were in my head, I was shocked to find how much negative self-talk my mind was engaged in. These were awful things that my mind was saying to me about me. I wouldn't tolerate anyone else saying even one tenth of that to me, yet it came from my most intimate space: my mind. No wonder I ate so much junk food.

If I were to succeed at replacing my addiction to junk food, I would need to put the diffusion tool at the forefront of my efforts.

Then, with the help of a friend on an online forum, I identified two powerful emotions for which I needed extra help. The diffusion tool alone wouldn't be enough for them.

First was anger. Anger resulted in an overwhelming need to binge eat hot pockets. I got angry a lot.

I realized I needed some space to calm down before applying the diffusion tool to anger. For this, I enlisted the help of my friend Steve. He had a way of listening calmly and patiently to me when I would rage about a situation. As a result, I felt calmer and able to see things more logically after talking to him. So, I asked if I could call him when I got angry during the next 90 days. He said, "Yes."

Next, I turned to dealing with hopelessness. I was now unemployed for two years after graduate school, living at my mother's home without an income. I preferred being homeless to having a job I hated, but I'd much rather have a job I could love that allowed me to contribute to the world. Feelings of hopelessness that I'd ever land a good job came regularly. Thus, that created an overwhelming need to binge on junk food.

After trying several tools, I found visualization to be the best. I found that if I felt hopeless, I could start visualizing the life I'd love to live. The hopelessness would disappear when I did that, and I'd feel hopeful instead. The need to eat junk food would then go away. I set on using this tool during my lifestyle change trial.

Now that I had found ways to deal with the emotions, I needed to deal with the psychological aspect of changing my habits. It would be intense, and I needed all the help I could get.

I considered whether I should do it gradually or have cheat days once a week. That might work for others, but I knew it wouldn't work for me. I needed to be all in. The idea of going big was more exciting and would help me marshal more energy to make it happen. I was also still under the 90-day deadline to change my cholesterol levels.

I set on using all the tools I used to remove the Coca-Cola habit five years earlier, and I added a few additional ones.

First, while I had my primary powerful "why" (the value of freedom), I felt I'd need to set up a backup motivator. The backup motivator would be a way to motivate me if, during difficult days, I couldn't connect to my primary motivator. The backup motivator would be a physical gift, a reward for completing 30 days. I set my eyes on an out-of-print board game called Star Wars Risk. My mother agreed to buy it if I made it to Day 30.

Second, I devised a mantra to keep me strong when looking at food while shopping. It was: "Nothing tastes as good as freedom feels." The idea was to repeat the mantra while food shopping and drone out temptations to load my cart with the usual junk food.

Third, I looked at all the possible ways this trial could fail. I made many contingency plans. For example, I played board games one weekend a month with a group that provided free cookies and chips. I planned to bring fruits and nuts so I wouldn't be tempted to eat the free potato chips. I also asked my mother not to store any junk food or processed carbs in the fridge for the first 90 days. That way, I wouldn't have any temptations at home. She agreed.

Second Attempt

After 12 days of intense research and preparation, I relaunched my lifestyle change.

Initially, it felt like I was walking a narrow beam high in the sky. One slight deviation, and I would fall crashing down. I had to stay very focused to stay on that metaphorically narrow beam. It felt intense.

In the morning, while showering, I'd visualize being successful at lowering my triglyceride numbers. I'd also visualize being able to travel around Asia while being healthy.

After a few days, I had an idea of how to experience the ice cream texture I loved without eating ice cream. What if I microwaved frozen fruits until they were soft but still cold? I tried it. It worked! The texture was cold, smooth, and sweet, like ice cream! I adored it. It became my replacement for ice cream.

I also started to feel waves of emotions. Waves of sadness, disappointment, and frustration buried for years began to surface. I used the tools of diffusion to allow myself to experience these emotions. I felt a sense of being centered while allowing these emotions to wash over me.

On Day 7, I wrote in my journal:

> *"Ok. Major potential crisis averted. I walked [from the source of anger] and called Steve up. Talked to him for 15-20 minutes. Was good. Helped to talk to him. He just listened. I felt better and realized I was stressed..."*

One day, halfway through the 30-day trial, I couldn't feel motivated to continue. It was so hard and required so much focus. Why was I doing this again? I couldn't connect to my primary motivation. Then I remembered my backup motivation: getting that out-of-print Star Wars Risk board game if I made it to Day 30. I felt motivated again and kept on going.

I soon had another challenge. I was scheduled to volunteer for five days as a vendor at a board game convention called BGG.CON. Two thousand people would be attending. It was at a hotel conference area. I figured there'd be so much junk food all around that healthy choices would be few. How could I stay healthy and stay on my trial? If I got hungry around all that junk food, that would be dangerous.

To solve that problem, I brought a cooler containing all my daily food. That way, I wouldn't depend on the hotel food or risk getting hungry. That included a veggie Subway sandwich and ample grapes, bananas, nuts, and water. It worked out great. During the four days of the convention, I kept on eating healthy. I even shared some of my grapes and fruits with other people.

As the days and weeks went on, I sometimes continued to crave junk food. I did not give in to it. I used the diffusion tool to allow myself to feel the craving without giving in to it. It was a novelty to realize I could feel a craving without obeying the command to eat it.

I also noticed that when I had cravings for sweets or hot pockets, there was usually some emotional disturbance within me that I hadn't yet processed. Once I processed the emotions and dealt with the issue, I noticed the craving would disappear.

Eventually, I stopped feeling like I was walking on a narrow ledge high in the sky. Instead, over time, I started to sense that my path was closer to the ground. My path also felt broader, with more room to maneuver before risking a crash. I still had to stay focused, but not as intensely.

Around day 23, I ordered the Star Wars Risk Game that I had my eyes on as my backup motivator. I wanted it to be there, ready to be opened up on day 30.

On Day 30, I rewarded myself by opening the Star Wars Risk Game. That backup motivator had proved crucial during difficult early days.

I still had more to go until I got tested for my cholesterol levels. I also wondered if this lifestyle was psychologically self-sufficient. Could I continue this long-term without using willpower? I didn't yet know. I knew it would need to be self-sufficient if I had any hope of making it last long term.

Results

On Day 63 of my 2nd attempt, I was called back to the doctor's office to get tested. A week later, the nurse called with the results.

She rattled off a bunch of different cholesterol numbers, but there was one I cared about the most: triglycerides. The test showed it at 146 - a significant decrease from 316 and below the 149 it needed to be. The other cholesterol numbers were also down from their dangerous levels. They were all in the safe zone.

I had succeeded. I was free.

What some said was impossible, I had made possible. What I struggled with for years, I had overcome. As a result, I had a second chance at healthy living.

By the 90-day mark, I felt younger, more energetic, and moved around faster than before. Gone were the days of laying on the couch like a beached whale after a binge-eating session. Gone were the days of having to walk slowly all the time. Gone were the days of feeling old.

Before starting the lifestyle change, I lacked the energy to spend a whole day at the board game-playing conventions. Now I did. Before the 90 days, I felt slow in calculating the math in board games. After 90 days, I saw that I was much faster at making math calculations in my head.

After 90 days, I knew I'd never want to go back to that previous lifestyle. And I haven't.

I also committed to continuing it for at least five years. After five years, I just continued on.

At the five-year mark, my triglycerides were at 78. A year after that, it was at 68, about 20 percent of what it was before the lifestyle change.

In November of 2022, I celebrated ten years without a single bite of ice cream, cheese, pasta, hot pockets, pizza, cakes, cookies, sweets, French fries, fried foods, junk food, and almost all processed carbs.

My life became so much better as a result.

Postscript

Five years after my lifestyle change, I achieved my dream of traveling to Asia. I did it while staying healthy.

My Reflection

I have been so incredibly grateful my younger self made this change. It gave me vitality, energy, and confidence to make more changes in my life. It helped me grow more into who I wanted to be. It also helped me become more aligned with the heart and more potent in my actions.

That's not to say everyone should give up all those foods I've stopped eating. Or that growth or living from the heart required such a dramatic lifestyle change. It does not. Eating all those foods in moderation while still being healthy and processing emotions is possible. For example, I never had a problem with being addicted to sausage and bacon, nor drinking wine. So,

105

sometime after the initial few months of my lifestyle change, I allowed myself to eat sausages and bacon and drink wine occasionally. However, for the rest of the food I avoid, I know it was the best decision to remove all of it for me.

It was better for me to 100% give up the food I was addicted to rather than just 99%. If I allowed myself "cheat days," then the temptation to eat that junk food would always be there. That would eat up precious conscious energy managing the temptation. I forgo any temptation by giving those foods up 100% of the time. My conscious energy could instead focus on other projects or areas to grow.

The great thing about making this habit change self-sufficient psychologically was that I didn't need any willpower or discipline to maintain it. Initially, I needed intense willpower to carry out the changes, but it has become a part of my life.

The food I used to be addicted to no longer felt like food fit for humans. I didn't mind if my family and friends ate it during our meals together. I would feel like I was watching a human eating strange alien food not meant for humans. It didn't bother or tempt me.

Here are some of the tools that helped:

- Using a backup motivator such as a physical gift to myself. If, at some point, I couldn't connect to my primary motivator, I could draw energy from my backup motivator.
- Asking for cooperation from others to remove all temptations for the initial part of the habit change trial.
- Coming up with a mantra to help me remind myself of what I was going for when I would be in the area of greatest temptation.

Your Reflection

What is one of the most challenging habit changes you've made?

What tools or methods did you use that helped you make that change successful?

What roadblocks did you encounter, and how did you circumvent them?

Chapter 10

Upgrading Identity
The Story of 5K's

I knew I was in trouble when, after almost one year of training to run a 5K, I couldn't even run three minutes straight. It was November of 2013. Since January of that year, I have been training with the goal of running in a 5K race by December. Somehow, despite going outside to train, I never made much progress.

The massive lifestyle change I had undergone the previous year (see previous chapter) had given me a new lease on life. I felt I had a new chance to live healthily. I wanted to make the most of that chance. Part of being healthy was exercising. I thought I could do that again since I had run thirteen years earlier while in college.

But after 11 months of trying to train, I had utterly failed. What could I do? I still wanted to enter that December race. One of my friends said, don't enter that 5K race; you'll just embarrass yourself by coming in dead last.

However, I decided that my goal had been to run in a 5K race by the end of the year. If I can't run the 5K, at least I can walk it. So, I signed up for the "Jacob Logan 5K" race. It was in honor of a teenager named Jacob Logan, who tragically died while swimming in a lake. The proceeds would go to a charity run by his parents.

I showed up to the race. The clouds were gray, and it was drizzling. A lot of teenagers were there, classmates of Jacob. They helped with the organization of the race. Many of them were also preparing to run in honor of Jacob.

I felt so touched just to be surrounded by the energy there. There seems to be a feeling of anticipation before the race. A feeling of people getting ready to go all out and do their best. It felt magical to me. I loved it.

While waiting at the starting line, I positioned myself in the back as I'd be mostly walking. I decided on a few goals:

1.   Finish the entire 5K
2.   Finish while standing upright.
3.   Finish without being dead last.
4.   Finish ahead of any 60+ year-olds

When it was time, the announcer said, "Go!". Runners started running hard. I walked. A few other people walked as well. I ended up sprinting a few times here and there. After turning the final corner, I saw the finish line. I ran to the end. I finished the race in 46 minutes and 49 seconds.

A few people finished after me, but not many. Out of 315 people who completed, 298 finished faster than I did. Only 15 people finished slower than I did. I wasn't dead last, but I was close. However, I was dead last out of the 15 men in my age group who completed the race.

Looking at the results, I realized I achieved three of my four goals. I had finished the 5K (Goal 1) while standing upright (Goal 2) and wasn't dead last (Goal 3). However, finishing ahead of all 60+ year-olds (Goal 4) was utterly shattered. Most 60+ year-olds completed the race faster than I did. Many, much faster.

After the race was over, the group of finishers all gathered under the pavilion. That helped us dry while the rain fell around it. Then, I saw the announcer announcing the first, second, and third place for each age group. They called out the names, and then the person came to claim their shiny medals. I saw smiles on the faces of the medal receivers. I also heard the applause each time a name was announced.

I felt so inspired. I didn't feel embarrassed, as my friend warned me. I felt inspired by seeing the winners claim their medals after a hard-run race.

When it was over and it was time to go home, I kept on feeling inspired. It had been a privilege to participate in the 5K. I also wanted to become one of those runners receiving a medal for placing in the top three of their age group. I didn't know how, but I was determined to do what it would take.

Identity

I started journaling to examine why I had failed to train myself despite trying for the whole year. I had, after all, succeeded in college. Why not now? As I journaled, I realized I didn't see myself as a runner or an athlete. I hadn't run since that one year in college thirteen years earlier.

What does a non-runner do? They don't run. If I saw myself as a non-runner and non-athlete, running races would be like pushing a heavy boulder up the mountain. Doable but very hard. Almost impossible.

After contemplating the situation, I decided to adopt a new identity as a runner and athlete. If I saw myself as an athlete, I figured it should become natural for me to train and race.

I also figured my identity as an athlete wouldn't shift overnight. I would need to keep reinforcing that new identity until it became a part of who I was. I took a few actions right away to start strengthening my new identity.

First, I told my friends tongue-in-cheek that I scored in the top 92% of the 5K. I did better than eight percent of the participants! An athlete celebrates his achievements.

Second, I created a folder on my smartphone called "Athlete." That's where I placed all the apps related to running and racing. Each time I looked at my phone, I was subconsciously reminded of this new identity I was adopting.

Third, I figured an athlete would compete regularly, so I entered races regularly. No more waiting 12 months. I thought about trying to race once a month so I'd have feedback to see where I'm at. Whether prepared or not, I wanted to put myself to the test like I imagined an athlete would. I signed up for my next 5K the following month in January.

Limiting beliefs

While working on my new identity, I realized I had a limiting belief that "exercising and doing 5K runs was dangerous to my health due to not having insurance."

I couldn't afford health insurance at the time. I couldn't afford to go to the doctor for anything beyond a minor illness. I was still unemployed, living at my mother's house after graduate school and conducting my job search.

Therefore, that fear was causing me to resist training hard, as I didn't want to hurt myself.

Once I identified that fear, I researched ways to train safely, from stretching regularly to warming up and cooling down before and after runs. I decided to become a super careful runner, paying close attention to what my body told me. I became reassured. My limiting belief disappeared as I felt I could now run safely.

I journaled to see if I had other limiting beliefs about running. I saw none. I was set to go.

Training

Now that I had started implementing my new identity and removed a limiting belief, I started researching "How does one train for a 5K race?" I found a lot of helpful information! Why hadn't I done this a year earlier? I was perplexed, but then I knew it was because I hadn't done the internal work yet.

I settled on a "Couch-to-5K" app that trains by alternating running and walking. Over the weeks, as the body adjusted, the app would increase the time to run and decrease the time to walk. I downloaded the app and started training in it. After one month, I made more progress than in the previous 12 months.

About a month after Jacob Logan's 5K, I showed up for my next 5K. It was held at a different park. The weather was bright and sunny. I came prepared to run in intervals alternating with walking. This time, I finished in 32 minutes and 35 seconds. That was an improvement of 14 minutes from the previous month. I was now running more than I was walking.

As I saw the improvement in my result, I started to wonder - could I run faster than I did 14 years earlier in college? Near the end of college, I had run in a 5K. The time of my 5K was around 26 minutes. I had also placed 2nd in my age group category.

How awesome would it be if I could run faster in my late 30's than in my mid 20's?

After the January race, I was supposed to race again in February. But February came and went by, and I hadn't raced. Same thing with March. I was still training but hadn't done a race by the end of March. I thought, ok, I really did want to be doing a race each month. So, I signed up for a race in April.

I raced a 5K in April and was excited to finish under 30 minutes at 29:16.

In May, I decided it was time to put in motion another part of my plan to adopt the identity of being an athlete. That plan was to join a running club that held races once a month. Not only would it be cheaper to run club races (significant to me as I was still unemployed), but I figured that an athlete hangs out with other athletes and competes with them regularly.

I showed up in May at a race organized by a running club called the Plano Pacers. I felt intimidated. *"Who was I to dare to think I could be one of them?"* I thought. But I figured that through osmosis, being there would help me adopt this new identity. I also thought being there would help me eventually run faster. I ran a 5K at the club's race and enjoyed it a lot, even though I was slower than the previous month.

In June, I returned to the club's next race, bought a year-long membership, and bought a shirt with the club's logo. I felt awkward the first few times I wore the club membership shirt on my training runs. *"Who was I to pretend to be one of those serious runners?"* I thought. However, I figured wearing such a shirt would help cement my identity as an athlete and a runner. Eventually, I felt comfortable wearing the shirt - and even adored wearing them on my training runs. My identity as a runner and athlete was solidifying.

I ran in four more races the rest of that year, getting faster and learning more about running, training, and racing. I still considered the goal of beating my college 5K time.

While attending the races at the racing clubs, I also started asking for advice from fast runners. What I learned about becoming faster was different from what I had thought. I started implementing their advice. It helped.

Thirteen months after that original Jacob Logan's 5K, I lined up to run at a race called the Dallas Running Club's Frigid 5K. The race was held near White Rock Lake in Dallas, Texas. It was in the 40s with cloudy skies. The running path hugged the cold water of the lake.

When the race started, I ran hard. I gave it everything I had.

When it was over, I looked at my watch. I saw I had run the 5K in 25 minutes and 18 seconds. That was faster than the 5K I had run in college. Thus, in my 30s, I ran faster than I did in my 20s.

I also won a third-place medal for my age group. I was proud of the medal, but I was prouder of having beaten the running time from my 14 years younger self.

Sitting in my car after the race, I reflected on how much I had changed. At how much running was now a part of my life. At how I was making the most of my second chance of living healthily. My core felt so touched by the transformation, especially after all the struggles I had in starting to run. I felt the tears running down my eyes.

Postscript

I continued racing, and in 2019, I ran a 5K race in 23 minutes and

23 seconds. That was less than half the time I finished that initial Jacob Logan's 5K race. I was in my early 40's too by then, so I had run a race faster in my 40's than I had in my 30's or 20's.

Within seven years of Jacob Logan's 5K, I had run in 64 races. That included many types of races, from one mile to five miles to half-marathons and sprint triathlons. The most frequent races, though, were 5K, my favorite distance.

My Reflection

A few years after I started racing, I was going through an intense process of interviewing for my dream job. I applied the mindsets I had developed through racing to the interview process. It helped me stay calm and channel my energy to be at my peak performance on interview day.

On the day of my big interview, I wondered, "How do people who don't race manage to go through the stress of such a high-pressure interview?". I knew I wouldn't have been able to handle the pressure of the interviews had I not repeatedly faced the pressure of running races.

Maybe that's why I felt called to run races over and over. Maybe my heart knew I'd need to train to run races to apply myself professionally. I can't say for sure, but I'm so grateful I did. In any way, running and racing met my need for competitive fun and kept me healthy.

Once I started working full-time again, running helped me deal with the stress and calm my emotions. I don't know if I could have succeeded at my new job without the outlet that running provided.

So, what does learning to run have to do with learning to live from the heart? Everything. We are on Earth through our physical bodies, and everything we do requires a physical body. The more active our bodies are, the more energy we have to live from our hearts. The more energy we have, the more we can show up for the world and love. That's not to say exercising is required to live from the heart—it's not. However, I found it helps me so much.

Your Reflection

What is a new habit you adopted that required you (consciously or unconsciously) to change your identity?

How did you go about making the change?

Here are some questions you can ask yourself that may help you with installing a new habit:

- What kind of person carries out this new habit effortlessly and naturally?
- What kind of identity do they have?
- What kind of actions can you take to install the identity of that kind of person over time?
- What can you do to remind yourself of that new identity?
- Where can you meet and hang out with people with that identity?
- What part of you is resisting adopting that new identity?
- How can you address that resistance, so it is no longer blocking you?

Building Resilience

"You can't change how people treat you or what they say about you. All you can do is change how you react to it."

Mahatma Gandhi

Chapter 11

Living Life on My Terms
The Story of the Bearded Man's Way of Life

(This story takes place about three to four years before the Green Wig Events)

I was at my wit's end several years after graduating from college. I had just turned 28 years old.

When I graduated from college with my bachelor's degree, I had both a degree and several years of experience as a software engineer in the aerospace field. But I walked away from that highly lucrative career to try to make a difference in the world.

I failed massively. I worked in a series of low-paying retail and factory jobs for four years. I had few friends and spent most of my time alone after work.

I had tried over and over to succeed. To get into a better situation. To fix the mess of my life. But to no avail. Life was shitty. Somehow, I had fucked up, and I didn't know how to get back up.

I felt so depressed. And years of trying to get out of this shitty situation and failing to do so led to nowhere but more misery. I felt hopeless I could do anything to change.

I decided to end my prolonged misery by ending my life.

However, my mother, who didn't know what I was planning, had planned to visit me in 30 days. She was going to drive over 730 miles to see me.

I thought it wouldn't be nice to kill myself before her visit. So, I decided to wait until after her visit to end my life. That seemed to be the nicer thing to do.

So, I found myself with only 30 days to live.

I didn't tell anyone of my plan. I lived in an apartment with a roommate. I worked at a Target store, moving boxes around the backroom. I hated my job, but I decided to keep going to work. I needed to pay my bills and keep up "appearances."

With only 30 days left to live, I immediately let go of all the intense pressure I felt to be successful. No longer would I feel like I was banging my head against the door, trying to succeed. I felt immediate relief.

Then, I asked myself: "How can I make the best of my limited time left on Earth?"

That question saved my life. Here's how it played out:

Day 1

For breakfast, instead of trying to eat a healthy meal, I thought, "*screw it. It doesn't matter anymore if I'm healthy or fat or how long my body can last on Earth. I've only got 30 days left to live. So, let's eat all the junk food I enjoy eating!*" I ate a Snickers bar and some M&Ms and drank a Coca-Cola for breakfast. Then, I planned on eating potato chips and some chocolate Twinkies for lunch.

As I arrived for my shift starting at 4 a.m., I looked at the electronic handheld device to see which set of boxes in the back room I needed to either pull from the shelf…or add to it. I selected a group and got to work.

Before being hired to work at Target, I had worked on a factory floor, helping assemble items. A coworker started arguing when I refused to do what he asked. He then punched me I started punching him back. We fought until management separated us. Thankfully, the police were not called. However, that was my last day working there.

I was OK with taking a punch. I knew how to deal with that. But I was not OK with losing my job.

When I started working at Target, I was scared of getting into disagreements with my coworkers. I didn't want to get into a fistfight and lose my job again. Plus, I figured there was no way Target wouldn't call the police if a fight broke out. So, I let my coworkers walk all over me. They constantly told me what to do and moved me from one area to another. Even after working there for a year, they kept directing me around. I felt bullied around. I hated it.

One day, a group of us were standing around and talking. One of them told me in front of the others that I didn't have a spine. I didn't disagree with his assessment.

But now that I had only 30 days to live, I thought "*screw that. So be it if I got into a fistfight again and lost my job. I wasn't going to take any more shit from anyone.*"

Later that day, I was pulling items in the backroom grocery area when a short, red-haired female coworker walked in. She said she was going to work in that section. I knew it was her favorite spot to work. She ordered me to go elsewhere. Until that day, I had always complied.

However, for the first time, I told her, "No. I'm working here."

She was surprised. She voiced her displeasure and repeated her demand. I repeated calmly, "No."

She went away and worked somewhere else. I felt I had won a little victory.

Day 2

As I got ready for work, I looked at my electric razor. Since I had started growing facial hair ten years earlier, I had always wanted to grow a beard. I had been too afraid to do so.

At the time, it seemed like the only people who had beards were homeless, unemployed bums. Everyone else was clean-shaven, with maybe a mustache or a goatee. As a teenager, I told Uncle Pierre I wanted to grow a beard. He told me there was no way I was to have one. If I did, I would be ridiculed and ostracized.

Later, as a 28-year-old, I was also told that women didn't like men with beards. I already had such a hard time dating, and I didn't want to make it more difficult.

But now that I only had 30 days to live – I thought, "*screw that. If I got ostracized, so be it. If I didn't date anyone, so be it.*" I wasn't dating anyone anyway. I wanted to finally see what it would be like to have a beard. So, I put my shaving kit away and went to work without shaving.

Day 3

I was pulling some bulky items when a couple of young male coworkers approached me. They told me to stop what I was doing. They asked me to walk to the other side of the store, pick up some boxes, and stock those.

I replied, "No, I'm working here now." The two coworkers seemed surprised. They had always seen me be compliant. They tried again to convince me to go. I stood my ground. They gave up and moved on. I felt satisfied with that outcome.

When I went home that day, I made another decision. Since I only had 30 days left to live, I didn't have to struggle in my free time to become successful. So, I would make the most of my free time outside work!

I was playing an online game that involved moving a tank and a little green man. I competed against other players with a tank and a little green man. I decided to be creative and create a graphic mod for the game. This would allow players to play the game while it looked very different. I had never done this, but I figured trying would be fun. It would also be something I'd leave for others to enjoy once I was gone. I started diving deep, devoting most of my free time to this graphic project.

Day 5

I was stocking items at the store when another male coworker directed me to work elsewhere. He wanted my spot. I said, "No, I'm working here.". However, he kept insisting I go elsewhere. He wouldn't take my "no". Finally, I walked off and went straight to find the manager.

After explaining the situation, I told the manager, "I'm willing to take orders from you, but I'm not willing to take orders from anyone else."

He agreed. He told my coworker to back off. Finally, I had won my peace. That was the last time a coworker from Target tried to bully me.

Day 7

I had gone almost a week without shaving. My beard was beginning to grow. I marveled, looking in the mirror, and enjoyed touching the hair on my face.

Day 10

One of the managers made a brief comment about my beard. It sounded like a note of approval.

Day 12

I had spent a week working at Target without interruptions or coworker attempts to bully me. I started to feel a sense of peace, knowing that whatever I started working on, I would see through to completion. I enjoyed the sense of achievement when I'd finish a batch. I also felt more self-respect, having stood up to my peers.

Day 13

I released my first graphic mod for the tank game: it turned a game set on a green island into a desert landscape. What had previously been grass was now sand. What had been trees was now cacti. The player's tank now looked 3D instead of a flat 2D image. Learning how to create and release it for other players was thrilling and captivating.

I had dived deep into learning so much about modifying graphic skins. It was so fun coming up with creative ideas and then playing around to see if I could make them happen. I was enjoying my free time so much.

Day 15

I had gone two weeks without shaving. What a beautiful, wild sight I saw when I looked in the mirror.

Day 18

I kept eating junk food. It was so nice not to stress about needing to be healthy.

Day 22

I had now gone three weeks without shaving. Despite my hair color being brown, my beard was red! That surprised me. Who knew? It was the only red hair on my body. I knew nothing about maintaining or trimming a beard, so the beard was growing wild. I didn't care. I loved it.

Day 25

I released my second graphic mod. This one was more ambitious. It turned the island landscape into a moon landscape. I used pictures of the moon to turn what was grass into moon dirt, replete with mini craters. The small boat that previously took the tank from island to island was now a tiny rocket ship. The trees were now pink energy crystals. What had been blue ocean water was now outer space with stars in the background. I had incredible fun using my limited graphic skills to create this fantastic-looking visual mod. I relished playing it. I had felt exhilarated the last 21 days working on the graphic mods.

Day 26

I was astonished that this job I hated so much had become enjoyable. Nobody bossed me around anymore. I got to start all of these work projects knowing I would be able to finish them. My coworkers left me alone.

I didn't love my job. But I enjoyed it now. I enjoyed the feeling of satisfaction from completing my tasks.

My beard was also growing wilder. I loved it.

As I drove home from work, I pondered my mother's looming visit and my plan to end my life afterward.

Did I really want to go through with it? Work had become enjoyable. I was doing fun things after work. I loved having my beard - it felt so "me." My stomach was starting to bulge from all that junk food I had been eating, but that was OK.

I still had many problems, but I was enjoying my life. Why not continue to live?

"However, if I stopped the plans to end my life, would my life return to being shitty and miserable again?" I thought, "yeah, probably."

I put the question aside and stayed focused on completing my plans.

Day 27

My mother told me she was bringing me a new computer. As soon as I heard that, I thought, *"OK, that's my excuse."* I couldn't possibly end my life now. I had something to look forward to. I would get to explore this new computer. Plus, life was feeling good.

So, I put an end to my plans. I decided to live.

In a way, I was already ready to live before my mother told me about the computer. After years of suffering and pain, I had just experienced a few weeks of living without massive pain. I had experienced some joyful living.

But I had been concerned that if I decided to live, I'd face an insurmountable mountain full of problems to overcome.

But once my mom told me about the computer, I felt like I had something to look forward to. It was like a silver light of hope coming through the stormy clouds ahead. The hope was that the good feelings I had now could continue even if I decided to live.

Day 30

My mother visited. We had a wonderful time together. She accepted and loved me even with my new wild beard.

Day 35

After she left, I opened a Word document on my new computer and wrote at the top, "The Bearded Man's Way of Life." It would be the manifesto meant for my eyes only. I wanted to take stock of the lessons I learned during those 30 days.

First, I wrote that "The Bearded Man's Way of Life" meant I would live life on my terms. I would no longer limit myself to doing what others wanted, nor would I listen to or live by their fears. No longer would I be restricted to doing what others approved of. If I resonated with doing something, then I would do it even if I faced the potential of significant backlash.

I would pursue my goals, doing what I desired regardless of what others thought was best.

Living by other people's rules had nearly killed me. Living on my terms and doing what was "me" gave me life.

Second, I wrote that the Bearded Man's Way of Life meant I would no longer take shit from other people. Instead, I would stand up for myself. I would refuse to be cowed. I would not allow myself to be bullied. Standing up to the bullies had made my job more enjoyable. It gave me life.

I also wrote that I was keeping my beard. Having a beard was so "me." I wrote that's how the Bearded Man lives - he does what he resonates with and deals with the consequences.

The beard became my private symbol to remind me of everything I had learned during those 30 days. Every time I saw myself in the mirror, it was a subconscious reminder to live life my way and stand up for myself.

Postscript

Day 120

I heard the song "Live Like You're Dying" by Tim McGraw for the first time. McGraw sings that he wishes everyone would have lived like they were dying to realize what's truly important about life. As I listened to the song, I realized that's exactly what I went through.

Day 932

I worked at Target for another three years. I became a trainer, mentoring new employees on the stock team. I also became a shift leader when my boss was off. When it was time to quit, my manager told me he'd need three people to replace me.

Over the years, my dating life seemed unaffected by my beard. On the contrary, dating became easier as I became more of the man I wanted to be.

Day 2,880

Eight years later, I made a successful lifestyle change to stop eating junk food, as that habit didn't serve me long-term.

Day 6,570

Eighteen years later, I still had my beard. It was still "me" and part of who I was. The difference is that the world seemed to have embraced beards. What was uncommon, rare, and shunned has become common, accepted, and celebrated. It shows the surprising way things can change in society.

My Reflection

My personal manifesto kept me driven and moving forward. It's gotten me to frequently make choices that aligned with my heart and soul, even if nobody around me agreed with them. That was the case even when it caused fear in other people and in me. In the long run, I was so much better for it. It gave me life—not just in terms of survival but also in terms of joyfulness.

Doing that also meant I could stand up to adversity in a way I couldn't before. It helped grow my resilience—my ability to face adversity.

However, playing with suicide ideation was like playing with Russian Roulette. I was lucky that I made it through. I wouldn't wish anyone else to go through this experience I went through. About 33,000 people die each year in America due to suicide. Worldwide, that number is 800,000 people annually.

I also know that thoughts of suicide enter at one point almost everyone's mind. Most people seriously consider it for at least two weeks during their life.

I eventually completely renounced suicide as a possibility for me, no matter what happened. I had noticed that my life's sweetest, most beautiful moments happened after my darkest, most challenging moments. Once I renounced the possibility of suicide, it never again became an option, even in moments of significant pain.

Your Reflection

What are the most hard-earned lessons that you've suffered to learn that you always want to make sure you keep in mind?

What do you do to remind yourself of those lessons?

Chapter 12

Embracing Obstacles
The Story of the Advantages

One day in 2013, I led a Toastmasters public speaking club as its president. In the audience was a man I had only seen once before. He was the division governor, two levels higher than I was. After the meeting, he asked me if I'd consider becoming an area governor. As area governor, I'd report to him and have four clubs to oversee.

I felt so honored to be asked. In all my years in Toastmasters, I had never risen above being a club president. I loved being president. I enjoyed driving my clubs to achieve the highest levels of distinctions possible—and had been able to do so at each of the three clubs I had been president.

I thought about what the division governor said. It would help me improve my leadership skills as now I'd be taking on a more significant challenge. I'd be helping 4 to 5 clubs reach their highest levels. It would probably be a lot of fun, too.

I told the division governor, "Yes." My term of office would last one year.

One of my duties was to organize area club contests, one in the fall and one in the spring. The winner of each club's speaking contest in my area would compete against each other at the area contest. Then, the winner of the area contest would go to the division contest and compete against the winners of other area contests. The contests would continue until one person won the Toastmasters world championship.

Putting on the area contest required a lot of coordination. I needed to secure a venue and secure donations of snacks and drinks. I'd need to secure contest judges as well as volunteers. I'd also need to ensure the clubs had their club contests so they could each send a participant to the area contest. I'd also need to have flyers made to market the contest, develop a theme, and so on.

I felt an extra added pressure as distinguished members of Toastmasters would be attending as well.

I had recruited my mother to be my assistant area governor. She had been so supportive by creating the flyer and helping with the logistics. However, one day, I saw something imperfect that she had done. I lashed out at her. I felt terrible about it afterward. The stress of it all was getting to me.

On the day of the contest, I showed up. Everything was in place. The snacks and food were there. The judges were there. The contestants, one from each club, were there. About 40-50 people filled the room. Once the contest started, I watched the contestants compete. It all flowed so well, with everyone doing their role well.

When it was over, multiple people, including the division governor, approached me to let me know how well-organized it had been. How well run it was.

But I was mentally exhausted. I was distressed by the experience. I had been so stressed out. I didn't know how I could do this again in the spring.

I had been proud to be an area governor. But I didn't think I could go through another stressful experience like that again. I wasn't concerned about how long it took: I had plenty of time as I was still mostly unemployed. But the stress of it was concerning to me.

I emailed the area governor to let him know I was quitting my role. He called back right away and talked with me. I couldn't take it anymore, so I confirmed that I was quitting my mid-term role.

I felt ashamed of it for years afterward. I had let people down. I had let myself down, too.

The Obstacle is the Way

Later the following year, I heard the author Ryan Holiday on a podcast by Tim Ferris. Ryan advocated for seeing obstacles not as something that blocks us but as something that helps move us forward with what we want. He quoted the Roman Emperor Marcus Aurelius as having written, "The impediment to action advances action. What stands in the way becomes the way.". Ryan used that quote as the basis for the title of his book, "The Obstacle is the Way."

After listening to that interview, I knew I had to get the book. I needed help dealing with obstacles. Once I bought the book, I immediately devoured it. The book contained many strategies and stories about using barriers to achieve goals.

As I read it, I felt so inspired. Until then, I saw each obstacle as something I had to grind through. Like a weight in front of me that I had to carry or push out of the way. Something that slowed me down. Something I had to push through painfully.

Life had felt so full of numerous daily obstacles. So full of weights, I had to pick up and move. It was exhausting pushing through it all.

While reading the book, I thought, *"how can I change how I deal with obstacles? How can I change my perspective on obstacles to stop lamenting (even silently) about them? How could I instead start thinking about how to use these obstacles to achieve my goals?"*

I figured if I could do that, it would help me become more resilient. Maybe it'd help me be less stressed out?

As I continued reading the book, I had an inspiration. What if I asked myself, "What is the advantage of this?" whenever I saw an obstacle? Both big and small obstacles. I didn't see that question in the book, but I thought that question might help remind me of everything I was learning in that book.

I became obsessed with the question, "What is the advantage of this?".

It reminded me of a conversation I had with a multi-millionaire friend. One day, he came home and saw his house burning unexpectedly. He asked himself how he could use that for his benefit. He proceeded to do just that. He took a disastrous event and made it into something useful for him.

So, I decided to ask that question hundreds of times for the next few weeks. I wanted to address all the obstacles in my life, big or small. I wanted to know if I could train myself to use obstacles as an advantage.

The next day, I was driving in slow traffic. I started complaining silently about how these cars were slowing me down and were in my way. I then stopped and remembered the question. So, I asked, *"What's the advantage of this traffic?"*

I thought, *"Well, I can practice feeling grateful that I have a car. Or I can mentally prepare myself for the steps to take at my destination. I can also use the time to listen to an educational audiobook."* That changed my perspective. I stopped complaining internally and instead used my time more effectively. I also felt relief, like I had put down the 20-pound weight I had picked up when I was complaining about the obstacle of the traffic.

That evening, I was watching TV. The remote control stopped working. I started to feel heavy, as if a weight had been put in my hands—yet another obstacle in a series of barriers to getting what I wanted. Then I remembered the question and asked myself, *"What's the advantage of the remote not working?"*

I thought, *"I could use it to grow more patient with technology. I could exercise by getting off the couch and going to the TV to change channels. Or I could use this as a reminder that maybe I could do something more productive with my time than watching TV."*

I felt the heavy weight on my shoulders lifted. The remote control not working could be my pathway to growing or doing something more important than watching TV.

The next day, I reflected on my employment situation. I was mainly unemployed, working only a few hours a week. I wanted a full-time job that I could love. I asked myself, *"What's the advantage of this?"*

I thought, *"I get to spend the extra time I have available going to workshops and learning how to land my dream job so I can have the kind of career I truly desire."* That lifted my mood. What was an obstacle (not working full-time) was something I could now see could help me land my full-time dream job.

Over the next few weeks, I asked that question hundreds of times. I asked that for all the small obstacles I could see, as well as all the significant barriers that loomed large. I asked that for the things that were immediately in front of me, as well as the things far out there. Anything that felt like an obstacle to having what I wanted, I asked the question, "What's the advantage of that?".

After those intense few weeks, I found I was habitually asking this question regularly. Not 100% of the time, but much more than before. I felt lighter and was able to see things from a fresher perspective.

Back in the Boiler Room

A couple of years later, I finally landed a full-time dream job at my dream organization. What I had identified earlier as an obstacle (not working full time) had indeed become a pathway to landing my full-time dream job.

After being hired, I felt it might be challenging even though I would love my job. It might be stressful. It might be difficult. Especially the first year.

I also knew I'd be incredibly tempted to quit. I had, after all, quit being a Toastmasters area governor despite loving the role. It wasn't the only time I had walked away due to the pressure and stress.

So, I made myself a solemn promise: No matter what, I would not quit this new job until at least my first anniversary. I wanted to give myself the chance to do this job. I felt it was critical to stay there as part of my path to working from the heart.

As I was onboarded into my role, I faced many challenges. There was so much to organize and clean up for my department, physically and digitally. The organization was also going through a significant expansion. Finally, I had so much to learn about the industry, the organization, and the people involved. It was a very demanding role, especially in the first year.

I loved it, though. I did my best to continue asking myself, *"What is the advantage of this?"* at every obstacle that came my way.

A few months after I started working there, the organization also hired Tom. Soon after starting to work, Tom began to forcefully tell me what to do. Despite being my peer, Tom wasn't shy about telling me how things needed to be done differently. I experienced him as a bully. His personality was pretty powerful and strong-willed.

The problem was that Tom and I had roles that meant we had to work closely together. We had to coordinate many things together. Instead, we clashed.

Our bosses saw the problems between us. They loved both of us and didn't want to let either of us go. Thus, they tried to get us to work better together. And both Tom and I tried hard to work together. But we weren't very successful. So many things in each of us triggered the other one.

Working with Tom in the office felt like carrying a 100lb weight. I didn't know if I could continue. I knew I felt like quitting. I didn't want to have to deal with Tom. That wasn't what I signed up for when I started this job. My dream job at my dream organization doesn't include working with someone like Tom. I felt so stressed.

What could I do? I didn't want to do anything to undermine Tom; that wasn't my place, my role, or the way I operate. So, I didn't. But I didn't want to be run over either. And I wanted to stay mentally ok and sane. In the end, despite feeling like quitting, I didn't want to stop. I had made that solemn promise to myself not to leave before my one-year anniversary.

I'd walk or run in the park every morning before work. At the park, I'd ask myself, *"What's the advantage of dealing with Tom and this situation?"*. I made it my mission to find an answer to this question every day. Since dealing with Tom was like carrying a 100lb weight on my back, I didn't want to add any more weight. If I was complaining internally about the situation, it'd be like adding more weight. I knew I'd break if I did that.

One day, the answer to the question "What's the advantage?" was that maybe I'd learn more about navigating complex people's problems. Another day, the answer was that it would help build resilience in me. Another day, the answer was: *"I can use this to become stronger. I can use this to grow and learn how to handle such volatile and stressful situations better. I can use this to help me overcome my triggers of people trying to bully me."*

I carried on, doing the best I could, reminding myself regularly of the benefit of dealing with this incredibly challenging and demanding situation. It was like walking through a powerful winter storm trying to knock me down. I stayed focused, regardless of how triggered I might be some days.

I usually tried to avoid walking by Tom's office. I'd take the long way around. But one morning, I happened to walk by his office. What I saw as I walked by stopped me in my tracks. His office was empty. It was now devoid of his many personal items. Apparently, Tom had come in early in the morning, taken all his stuff out, and quit without notice. I was shocked.

My powerful, strong-willed, domineering coworker, whom I had never imagined would quit, had just quit. He hadn't been able to handle the pressure or stress.

At our next staff meeting, our bosses and coworkers were sad. Tom had been an excellent, productive worker. But I had to suppress a smile. The 100-pound weight on my back had been lifted off.

More than that, though. While Tom had quit, I hadn't. I was no longer the guy who resigned when the pressure became high. I was no longer the guy who couldn't handle it. I was no longer the same man who had quit being an area governor.

I felt my identity made a shift. I was now the guy who could persist through a high-pressure situation while being ok and staying sane. I felt proud.

Postscript

The following year, Tom reapplied to work for the organization. Did he regret having quit? Despite having done impressive work, I was told he was not considered for one main reason: he quit without notice.

My Reflection

Working for the organization was one of the best things I've done. Despite and perhaps because of the challenges, I learned much about working from the heart. I also had many opportunities to transcend other issues. I learned a lot about working with powerful, heart-centered leaders. Finally, I made many incredible connections that I have treasured during my time there.

The question "What's the Advantage of this?" has been a game changer for me. It's not the only thing that has helped me overcome obstacles. However, it has been critically important to help redirect my focus in a way that is both helpful and helps me overcome the obstacles.

That's not to say we shouldn't quit when something isn't working. That's not to say quitting is automatically a bad thing. It's not. There are times to stop and leave. Otherwise, we're wasting time, energy, or money. This is especially true when it's mentally affecting us. It's better to stay sane and leave than to stay in and lose ourselves.

However, I knew that living and working from the heart meant that sometimes the going gets hard. It's not always all flowery and games. Hard conversations need to be had, hard decisions need to be made, and complex challenges must be navigated.

The better prepared my mindset was to deal with challenges and adversity, the better I could navigate life from the heart.

Your Reflection

Looking back at times when you dealt with adversity better than at other times, what made a difference for you? What did you do differently?

What level would you rate your resilience (ability to deal with adversity) from one to ten, with one being the lowest and ten being the highest?

How do you feel about the answer?

Chapter 13

Diffusing Triggers
The Story of Button Love

In 2013, after many years of my social life being mainly online, I felt it was time to change that. I sensed that the next step in living from the heart was to create a local in-person social life. To make in-person local connections.

At the time, I had been living in Dallas, Texas, for a little over a year. I was still unemployed, looking to start a new career while living at my mother's place. Thus, I had no regular outlet to meet people. I did play at a weekly board game meetup. However, most of the time, I just played games without socializing much. Beyond that, I didn't have any local connections.

The desire was there, but unfortunately, I felt incredibly anxious to meet new people. I looked regularly for local meetups and would sign up for them. Then I'd keep canceling going to them or just not show up.

I finally attended a Chinese language meetup at a local restaurant. I knew a few Mandarin words, but not many. I was curious about learning more. I thought it'd be interesting to see what happens.

When I showed up, I sat at a table with four or five people attending the meetup. Some attendees were fluent Mandarin speakers, but the rest were learning. One of the native speakers quizzed me on what I knew. He repeatedly emphasized, "You need to learn more before you return.".

Outwardly, I nodded and didn't say anything. But inwardly, it was like a dagger stabbing me. He was saying I didn't belong there as I knew too little. I swallowed the effect and pretended that it didn't bother me.

However, once I was home, I felt much pain about the whole experience. The pain was around my heart and gut area. I tried to reason logically that it wasn't a big deal. But for several days, I felt the pain. It twisted and gnawed on me. As a result, for a few days, I didn't want to deal with anyone. I also never went back to that meetup nor learned any more Mandarin.

That was such a massive problem for me. I could be so easily triggered. A straightforward sentence someone said could result in me being in pain for days. I didn't know how to deal with it. Reasoning logically didn't help. Swallowing didn't help. Isolating and avoiding people was the only thing that could help. I felt super anxious about meeting new people, knowing each time I met with people, I could be in pain for days.

Isolating myself was no longer how I wanted to live my life. I wanted the freedom to attend local meetups, meet new people, and feel fine afterward. I didn't want to risk pain anymore. I didn't want to only rely on meeting people online anymore. Meeting people online was safe, as I could control things much easier. But if I would continue to grow in living from the heart, it was time to move beyond that.

I wanted to claim freedom for myself. Freedom from people triggering me. Whether on purpose or accidentally. I also wanted to give people around me the freedom to be themselves—and not feel like they have to walk on eggshells around me for fear of triggering me.

Ultimately, I wanted the freedom to connect; however, I wanted to connect. Freedom to live from the heart.

I had no clue how I'd get there. But I knew I wanted out of my prison of isolation and pain.

Inner Steel

There's a saying that the teacher will appear when the student is ready. That happened to me in 2014.

That's when Erin-Ashley Kerti, whom I had met at a personal development workshop a few years earlier, released a free tool on her website called "Inner Steel." The tool was for sensitive people who got triggered regularly. The tool was aimed at helping to process triggers.

I downloaded the PDF that describes the tool. Then I read it. I decided to try it out on something someone said recently that was bothering me.

First, I selected the phrase that had recently triggered me. I opened a notepad on my computer and wrote the phrase where I could easily see it. Then, I chose one of the five physical power poses. Finally, I set a timer for 5 minutes.

While in that power pose, I looked at the phrase. Then, I allowed whatever feelings and thoughts to come up. Slowly, the sting and the pain started defusing and reducing itself. By the end of the five minutes, the phrase that had been stinging me…felt utterly neutral! Then, per the instructions, I wrote down some of the wisdom I had learned from doing this.

I was blown away at how effective that was. I loved it. I didn't have to spend a few days in pain!

That also seemed a whole lot better than simply "swallowing" or burying the pain inside as I used to do before. Seemed healthier and much faster.

OK, so that worked for one trigger. But how many triggers did I have? Dozens? Hundreds? Maybe a thousand? How could I defuse all of them? How could I eliminate all these triggers so I could experience freedom?

I thought there was no way I would do this in a day, a month, or maybe even a year. I figured that, at worst, I probably had a thousand triggers. That is, a thousand things people could say that would trigger me, push my buttons, and cause me to react defensively or feel hurt. So, what if I set to work on diffusing one trigger a day for three years? I calculated that would result in defusing 1,095 triggers. That felt doable as it was only five minutes on average a day. Maybe by the end of the three years, I'd experience the freedom I desired?

OK, I liked that a lot. But how am I going to stay focused on this? Three years is a long time to stay focused on one exercise. There could be so many distractions along the way. So, I considered making it a game and thus keeping track of it. I also thought keeping track of my statistics would help make it fun. That would then help me stay engaged with it in the long run.

Button Love

So, in November of 2014, I opened an Excel spreadsheet. I set up three columns. In the first column, I labeled: "Date" for the date of the triggering incident. In the second column, I marked

"Phrase/Comment" for that which would trigger me or push my button. The third I labeled "Wisdom" that would result from applying the Inner Steel Process.

Then, I set up an Excel formula to track my progress. The formula listed:

1. How many I had done so far
2. How many I was doing on average per day
3. How many I have left to achieve my overall goal

The formula would automatically update the stats each day.

My goal: Processing an average of one trigger per day for about three years for a total of 1,000 buttons.

I called the process "Button Love," or "BT" for short.

I wondered: Would it work? Would I be able to transcend all of these triggers so that I could gain my freedom?

With my spreadsheet and my process ready, I started.

The first week, I worked on the triggers for an average of one daily.

When talking with someone, if I noticed an adverse reaction within me, I'd make a mental note of it. It could be an anxious feeling, irritation, or annoyance triggered by what someone said. Then, once back home, I'd write it down on the spreadsheet. Sometimes, I'd be triggered multiple times in the same conversation. I'd write it all down after the event.

That made being triggered almost fun because it meant I had uncovered another button I'd get to work and transcend.

Then, when I was alone, I'd work on the button. I'd write the phrase on the notepad on my computer, place myself in a power pose, and set the timer for five minutes. Some days, I'd work on a couple of buttons. On other days, I didn't work on a single one. But I'd check my BT stats almost daily to check my progress. If I saw I was in danger of averaging less than one button a day, I'd catch up. If I was ahead, I'd relax a little bit. Ultimately, I rarely went more than two days without working on a single button.

Keeping a list of triggers to work on turned out to be easy. I was triggered quite often. Since I could uncover triggers only by interacting with people, it motivated me to go out and meet with people. Thus, I started attending more meetups.

I felt like the boxer Rocky Balboa. Rocky was training his muscles day in and day out to get ready for his match. I was aiming to train my nervous system to be calm regardless of what others may say.

By the first anniversary of starting the BT process, I had uncovered, processed, and dissipated about 365 triggers, averaging one a day.

As I worked through trigger after trigger using the Inner Steel Process, I found it was highly effective for about 95% of what triggered me. For the other 5%, I'd need to do deeper inner work. Doing the Inner Steel Process was still beneficial as it calmed me down and gave me space to do the deeper work.

Day by day, I hadn't noticed significant changes in my life. However, I enjoyed the challenge of keeping my average of triggers processed at one per day. I liked knowing I was making progress.

However, by the one-year mark, I saw significant changes. I saw how my social life had evolved significantly. I attended more events and started integrating myself into some of these communities. For example, I became the race director for a small monthly race at one of my running clubs. I made more intimate friends at the board game clubs and enjoyed my time there even more. I also joined a spiritual community for the first time ever. I attended events there and made more friends. I also started participating in circles of men.

I also started networking and becoming friends with other professionals looking for jobs. This allowed me to receive meaningful feedback about improving my resume and job search. Thanks to the BT process, I stayed open and accepted this feedback. That made a big difference in my job search.

But best of all, my anxiety levels with meeting new people dropped significantly. I stopped feeling like I was risking days of pain each time I met someone new. I now knew I could meet new people and feel fine afterward.

I started working full-time about a year and a quarter into the Button Love process. Soon after, I stopped the BT process. I felt complete. I had processed 400 triggers by then. I didn't sense the need to continue.

I had gained my freedom. The freedom of being able to connect locally. The freedom from being triggered so much by what people said or did. The freedom to be more of who I wanted to be and do the things I wanted to do. The freedom of living more from the heart by connecting more with others.

My Reflection

Becoming much more connected to the local communities helped me live more from the heart. As I felt more connected (and worked through my inner issues), my joy and happiness increased significantly beyond what I had ever experienced.

That increased my resilience, not only in terms of being less triggered by people but also in terms of building my social network. Studies have shown that having close friends and robust social networks helps build resilience. That's due to the power of human connections. Humans are, after all, social animals. Because of the increased human connections I experienced, I became more resilient at my new job and in dealing with other challenges.

That's not to say that I became 100% free of triggers. I didn't. Sometimes, things came up. But it didn't cause lasting pain anymore. I could also process and deal with it quickly most of the time. And it didn't keep me from having the social life I wanted.

That's also not to say I didn't have further inner work to do regarding establishing a social life. Some years later, I went through another significant experience that helped me grow my ability to connect with others. Having done the BT process helped set me up to be ready for that future growth experience.

Your Reflection

How often do people say things that cause you to be annoyed, irritated, hurt, or defensive? How frequently do you get triggered?

When triggered, how do you react? Do you isolate yourself or try to strike out at others to control what they say around you, or a different way?

Chapter 14

Joining a Growth Community
The Story of Circles of Men

In 2014, after many years of participating in online personal growth forums, it was time to say goodbye to the forums. These forums had helped me grow significantly. I also met individuals like Josephine and Boniebelle, who had powerfully impacted and inspired me. I had learned so much that had helped me grow. However, I felt I had hit a plateau. I sensed that the next step to learning to live from the heart was to find local growth support groups. It's time to meet face-to-face.

So first, I said goodbye to the group. Then, I started to explore the local growth support group. Luckily, I lived in Dallas, so there were plenty of opportunities.

One day, I found a circle of men advertised on meetup.com. ManKind Project organized it. I went to visit them.

I showed up outside of a nondescript office building. I then went up the stairs to the second floor. Next, I walked into a room that was somewhat dimly lit. In the middle of the room stood 7-8 metal fold-up chairs arranged in a circle, facing inward. Five men were sitting in those chairs. After greeting the men, I joined in and sat down.

After one of the men described the confidentiality rules, we started the first round. During that first round, I experienced men expressing their feelings in a safe, masculine environment. When it was my turn to speak, I couldn't do that. I just said surface stuff like, "I'm fine." Feelings were things I had zero training in talking with other men. I had grown up in an environment where it was unsafe to talk about feelings. Especially to men. After that initial round, there were other rounds in which I could self-reflect and work on myself.

By the end of the first meeting, I was impressed. I loved the openness, the authenticity, and the self-exploration. I could tell the circle offered a lot of growth potential for me.

As a visitor, I could visit the open circle held twice a month. However, the group had a closed circle the other two weeks of the month. That circle would involve much deeper work. I wanted to attend that circle. I wanted to go deeper.

I told them I wanted to attend the closed circle as well.

One of the men, David, told me:

"Come to ManKind Project's 48-hour "New Warrior Training Adventure" weekend with us in the middle of Texas, about 3 hours from here. It'll be a great opportunity for you to grow, and you'll then be able to join the closed circles."

While he said that, I automatically translated it in my head. What I thus heard was:

"I want you, as a French man who obviously isn't from Texas and who spent time growing up in rural Georgia and got into fist fights with hostile local rural boys who were attacking and trying to hurt you, to leave the city and go to a rural area in the middle of Texas far away from civilization. There, you will spend the weekend on a compound with many local Texans you don't know. And on top of that, a man ended up killing himself after going to that event. So when can I sign you up for it?"

I thought, "*Yeah, no, thank you, absolutely not. I treasure my life too much.*"

Plus, the name didn't inspire me. "Warrior?" I didn't want to be a warrior. I wanted to be a lover.

So, I decided to stick to attending the twice-a-month open circle meetings. They invited me back.

I started attending the open circles regularly, sitting with about 5-8 men each time. Sometimes, I was the only guest; sometimes, there were other guests. I loved every single one of the meetings. I enjoyed the self-exploration. I also enjoyed spending time with these men as they remained in their masculine energy while at the same time being authentic and sharing their feelings, struggles, and growth. Going to these meetings grounded me.

The circles had a structure to it that worked very well for me. I always felt welcome to come back. They never pressured me to attend the New Warrior Adventure Training "NWTA" Weekend.

While sitting in these circles for ten straight meetings, or about five months, it slowly dawned on me that these men were good men. I started to trust them. I began to trust that these men wouldn't do anything intentionally to hurt a non-Texan like me. And if these good men spoke so highly of NWTA, then perhaps it could be safe for me to go. Good men wouldn't speak highly of a weekend training that did terrible stuff to men, right?

I very much felt the desire to attend the closed circles and do deeper work. To do that, I needed to do the NWTA first.

The evening after the 10th meeting, I went to David. I told him I wanted to sign up. He gave me a link to pay my fee. I had about three months to wait to attend the next NWTA. And there was a lot of paperwork to fill out.

I hated the paperwork. Not that I hate regular paperwork. But that specific paperwork for NWTA was odious to me. It made me nervous. So many personal details were required, and so many waivers needed to be signed.

Did I do the right thing by signing up for it? Was I foolish? Was I risking my life? I pondered these questions.

While waiting, I dug deeper online into NWTA and ManKind Project. I read the newspaper article about the man who attended the NWTA and then ended up killing himself afterward. That scared me. Would I want to kill myself after attending the NWTA?

When the organization was founded in the 1980s, they asked the men to keep what happened at the NWTA a secret. They wanted it to be like a movie experience with no spoilers for the new men.

That was great then, but now, with the Internet, it is impossible to keep such secrets. Thus, the men who hated it or had a bad experience were almost the only ones talking about it online. The men who loved and benefited from it would honor that tradition of staying mum. Thus, the information I found online was incredibly negatively biased.

I did find a page on the ManKind's webpage that said that men were now allowed to talk about the specific details of the training. However, the local men I knew stayed silent regarding the details of the NWTA. They simply expressed how much they loved it. That frustrated me.

I finally found an online forum with many details about NWTA. It was written chiefly by men who did not like their experience of it. It was scary stuff. Stuff about keys, wallets, and phones being taken away from each attendee during the weekend and only given back after it was over. Stuff about doing bare-your-soul type of emotional work in front of other men. And more.

About a month before the NWTA weekend, I almost backed out. But I calmed myself down.

Then, one week before going to the NWTA, I was taking a bath. In the middle of the bath, I thought, "*ok, this is ridiculous. I am not going to do this. I want to attend the closed circles but won't risk my life for that.*" I got out of the bathtub so I could put in a cancelation on the website.

Before I canceled, I decided to meditate for a few minutes. I sat, closed my eyes, and breathed deeply to calm myself. As I meditated, I heard my inner calm voice saying, "*Trust this. It will be good for you in the long run. You will be ok. Things will be fine for you if you go*".

Reluctantly, I put my computer away and backed away from canceling.

On the Friday of the event, I went to pick up the three other attendees I was tasked to pick up. The organizers of NWTA had asked us to carpool there. I volunteered to drive us. That way, I could get away from there and drive home if I wanted to leave in the middle of it.

As I drove to pick up the first man, I felt that fear running through me. I deeply breathed as I went, recognizing what a journey and growth I had been on to just show up to this event. I was choosing to trust myself and my decision to do this and face these fears.

Before I left, though, I scheduled a phone call with one of my closest friends. She was to call me the Sunday night when I returned. Her role was to check with me that I was ok and not suicidal. I didn't want to end up like that guy I read about in the newspaper.

NWTA

I picked up the three other attendees around Dallas, and we drove toward a tiny town called North Zulch in the middle of rural Texas. We had awkward conversations in the car.

Once we arrived, we drove into the complex called "Lands of my Grandfathers." After I parked my car, we got in the line of attendees to be processed.

As we were processed, I was asked to surrender my keys, wallet, and phone. I was also patted down, and my backpack was searched to ensure I had nothing else that needed to be surrendered. I was glad I knew this would happen. Otherwise, I would have freaked out, turned around, and left immediately.

I wanted to sneak in a pencil, though. I knew it was against the rules, so I hid it in one of the pockets of my bag. I wanted to have something to write in case I needed it. And I was curious if I could get away with it. Part of me doing my little rebelling against the rules. They never found it.

Once checked in, for the next 48 hours, I was on an intense journey called the Hero's Journey. The Hero's Journey, popularized by Joseph Campbell, is a structure where the hero embarks on an adventure, faces challenges, undergoes transformations, and then returns home. George Lucas based the first Star Wars movie on the Hero's Journey.

After the NWTA started, I participated in many exercises, some on my own and some in groups. I also got to reflect on my life's mission by journaling on my own. (Sometime after check-in, I was given a pen.)

Then Saturday afternoon came. It was the event I had read online that I dreaded the most, the part that seemed the scariest. The time to face a deep emotional wound. To face someone or something metamorphically that had hurt me. Time to go through the trials portion of the hero's journey.

To do this, we split into groups of 8-10 men, with a couple of facilitators helping each group. We would each take turns facing a deep emotional wound through a setup tailored to each man. Emotions were raw. It was hard work.

When it was my turn, I was asked what that wound was and how I might want to face it. I reflected on what I had seen other men go through in their trials. But as I listened inward on what I wanted to do, I realized I wanted to do something I hadn't seen any other men do yet.

I wanted to punch the hell out of my Uncle Pierre.

Uncle Pierre had been involved in raising me. Growing up, I felt dominated by him and grew up feeling I didn't have a choice in anything I did when I was in his care. I'd feel unfree and felt like I had to do things exactly his way, or I'd be in significant pain. It wasn't his way or the highway. It was his way, or you're gonna feel so crushed. He didn't physically abuse me, and he did provide for my sister and me. But I'd feel oppressed. And unloved. As an adult, I resented all of that.

That relationship with my uncle also tainted my relationship with anyone else who was also powerful and strongly assertive. Dealing with these assertive people brought up a lot of anxiety. It was as if they could immediately crush me. That went for both men and women. Thus, I avoided these kinds of people as best I could.

I wasn't scared of physical violence. Growing up and going through high school, and even once in my 20s, I had gotten involved in a few fistfights. I never threw the first punch or hit someone first. However, as soon as someone hit me, I'd immediately go into what I call my kamikaze mode. I didn't care how big the guy was or what the situation was; I would hit back with everything I had. Thus, I fought guys bigger than me, and I once fought two brothers at the same time. I never ran away when I was physically attacked.

But when it came to confrontation with strongly assertive people that did not involve any threats of physical violence, I'd be scared shitless. I didn't know how to handle them. I'd feel this impending sense of being crushed. And I'd feel powerless with a lot of anxiety. So, I did my best to stay away from such people.

However, I knew if I was to continue to grow and live from the heart, that meant I'd need to deal with such people. That meant dealing with my Uncle Pierre first.

And to me, that looked like punching the hell out of him. I wanted to reclaim my power from him. And I also wanted to punch him for not loving me.

I didn't think it would be possible. I still announced what I wanted to do. I was delightfully surprised when a staff member said, "Bring out the punching bag."

Out came the punching bag. One of the staff men picked it up and held it still.

I approached the punching bag. I then unloaded years of frustration, feeling oppressed and dominated into that punching bag that represented my Uncle Pierre. Years of feeling unloved by him. Each punch that landed was like me chirping at my power back. Each punch was an outflow of emotions that had been stored up and repressed within me. I unloaded in a very focused yet crazy all out manner on that punching bag. The man who held the punching bag up later said he was surprised at how hard it was for him to hold the bag with the force I was punching it.

After all my emotions went into the punching bag and I felt complete, I stopped punching the bag. At that moment, I saw a new truth and power within me. The new truth I adopted was that I would be capable of standing up to such powerful people. I had uncovered a new power within me to do so. And I also experienced love within myself, regardless of what Uncle Pierre said or did. As I sat down afterward to reflect, I experienced such a sweet moment of reflection as I absorbed what I had just experienced.

The rest of the weekend was a joyous celebration for me. I had done what I feared most and felt cheerful, happy, and grounded. I had been deeply emotionally vulnerable in front of men I had just recently met. I also saw many other men be deeply emotionally vulnerable with each other. I experienced how we all became stronger as a result.

When the NWTA was over, I received back my keys, wallet, and phone. As I drove the other three men home, we talked excitedly, having bonded during the 48 hours we spent together.

When I got home Sunday afternoon, I received the scheduled call from my friend, who checked on me to ensure I was ok. I verified I was very much ok and shared the beautiful realizations I got out of the weekend.

Post-NWTA

Many men take these NWTA weekends, have a good experience, and move on. But that wasn't why I took it. I wanted to join the closed circle.

After doing the NWTA, the men welcomed me into the closed circle. There, the real work began. The closed circle had all these powerful tools available. These tools were not available in the open circle. It requires men to be capable of emotional vulnerability and be deeply open. It required men to trust the other men in the circle that they were safe. For the most part, that required a man to have gone through an NWTA first.

And now that I had confronted Uncle Pierre metaphorically, I also knew I would need to face and confront him since he was still alive.

But not yet. I wasn't ready for that just yet. I needed to get prepared for it.

First, I went through a 6-week ManKind class called "PIT" to learn some of the tools used in the closed circles. One of those tools was expressing and processing my anger in a safe container.

That tool also revolutionized my life. I learned to stand in front of a man calmly and nonviolently and tell him I was angry at him and why. Then I could separate what part of that was projection (i.e., things that happened in my past that I was projecting onto this man) and what wasn't. Finding out what I was projecting and clearing that out eliminated the anger 90-95% of the time.

For a while, it seemed that each time I came to a weekly meeting, I ended up being angry at some man. And so I ended up doing the clearing process over and over. But what I was really doing, now that it was safe to express anger in that container, was that decades of unprocessed projections came out. Processing the anger and clearing away the projection almost every time would give me a sense of peace and incredible realization.

After doing a dozen clearings in the meetings with the other men, I realized I knew the process well enough that I could do it by myself. So, I started doing that on my own. Each time I got angry at someone, I processed myself with the clearing tool. I probably ended up doing it over a hundred times. After doing this consistently for a few years, I got angry so much less often. Over time, my life experience became much more peaceful.

However, before I got to that point, as I attended the circle of men meetings each week, I'd tackle whatever inner work was in front of me. I'd examine aspects of my psyche, belief structure, or how I showed up in the world. Then, I'd do the deep work while these men assisted me. Week after week. Months after months.

Uncle Pierre

After about six months, I felt it was time to confront my Uncle Pierre. No one suggested it. But I felt internally that it was time to do it. I wanted to stop pretending how I had been treated was ok. I thought it was time. First, I wanted to create a better relationship with him. Second, as the original source of my anxiety regarding strongly willed people, I figured confronting him would then in term help me stand up to and work with other very assertive people.

I hadn't seen him in person or talked to him on the phone for years. Instead, we had only communicated via email. I sent him my first email, describing some of my truths about what didn't work for me growing up. I knew he wouldn't like what I had to say.

He responded quickly. Uncle Pierre dismissed all the things I said didn't work for me, and instead, he wrote about how I should be grateful for all he did. As I read his response, I felt like my concerns were treated as worthless.

I started to feel that familiar feeling that the walls were closing in and that I was about to be crushed. I felt pain in my torso and felt the urgent need to run away from my computer.

I breathed deeply and let the email sit in my inbox. I didn't want to respond harshly or quickly. I took my time to process it, sort out what was said, and find my truth. The circle of men was there to help me process what was going on within me.

I also knew I risked my Uncle Pierre completely breaking off all contact with me. He had done this with other people in his life. At the same time, I wanted an adult-to-adult relationship. Not an adult-to-boy relationship that we had. I wanted to change the terms, and it was up to me to claim that. I felt that part of claiming that new relationship was to speak my truth about the past not being ok for me.

Thus, I decided to risk my relationship with him. I wanted to stay connected with him as he had been essential to my life. However, if he chose to disconnect from me forever because I voiced my truths, that would be his decision. Not mine. And I could live with his decision. I was seeing a bigger picture. To speak my truth to other strongly assertive people without feeling such an overwhelming sense of being crushed, I needed to start with my Uncle Pierre.

A few weeks later, I wrote back to him. I told him the truth about my experiences.

He wrote back right away. His email was as harsh as his first one. I breathed deeply and calmed myself down. As I processed his response, I saw for the first time the bullying tactics he used to try to get me to shut down. His email reminded me of a prominent bully-politician running for federal office at the time. This bully-politician would savagely attack anyone who opposed him to try to get them to shut down. I saw how my uncle's tactics had a lot of similarities with this bully-politician. Seeing the similarity in the tactics didn't make it easier. But it helped give me the space to step back and process what was happening within me.

I went back to the circle of men to help process this. I did more work and more reflection. Then, eventually, after some time, I wrote back. And he replied immediately, as harshly as before.

And so we started a cycle. I would take my time to process his emails, find the deeper truths within me, and work on them. Then, I'd carefully write back my uncomfortable truth to each of his points. Each time I wrote back, I didn't know if it would be the last time I'd hear from him. He would then write back, usually quickly and harshly, and use some form of bullying tactics against me.

I found it helpful because I could see the more profound and deeper layers as we continued writing. I saw more clearly the accusations my uncle would throw at me growing up. The fear of receiving that kind of accusation would then get me to be so obedient to him for fear of being crushed. Now, I could see those accusations on the screen. That meant I could take my time to process them. I could slowly dispel how they were untrue and simply a tactic to get me to comply.

The exchanges continued for over a year. Sometimes, it took me a few weeks to respond. Sometimes, it took me a few months. But answer, I would.

My uncle hadn't stopped responding to me. But he also hadn't seemed to accept much of anything I said. I hoped he would understand why things didn't work for me growing up. I eventually let go of that hope.

I realized it didn't matter how he responded. What mattered was that I spoke my truth and shared what I had been afraid to share. What mattered was how I spoke up for myself, both my past and present self. I reclaimed my power by speaking my truth instead of pretending that how I was treated had been ok when it hadn't been.

And so slowly, I claimed my place as an adult in that relationship. I didn't need him to acknowledge anything for that to happen. I instead needed to speak my truth and withstand his barrage back.

After a year or so of these exchanges, I felt complete.

After finishing our discussion, I invited him to visit me in the city where I lived. It would be our first time seeing each other in some years. We ended up spending a few days together. I experienced a change in the dynamics. Once, when I felt he stepped out of line, I pointed out that wasn't acceptable. That was such a massive shift for me to do that. We were no longer an adult male and a boy. We were two male adults. We ended up having a great time together.

The following year, I visited him and stayed at his place for a while. We had a good visit.

Then, several years later, I visited him for a month. He had moved to a new area I had never been to. After a few days there, I started noticing how I was feeling so disrespected by him. I'd find it disrespectful how he constantly interrupted me when I was talking. I also experienced how rude I'd be talked to when we had a different opinion, especially after he's had a few drinks. I wasn't used to any of that anymore. I was used to surrounding myself with people who tend to be respectful, even when we disagree on topics.

Why did I experience so much disrespect on this visit and not the previous visit five years earlier? I'm not entirely sure. Perhaps it's because I stayed pretty sober during this visit instead of drinking along with my uncle as I usually did. Or probably because my life had continued to evolve. I now had much more experience dealing with assertive and decisive people who treated me respectfully.

Regardless, the way my uncle was talking disrespectfully and harshly to me was something I usually didn't accept and tolerate from anyone. Yet here it was happening.

I pondered what to do about that. Out of the options I had available, I settled upon one. I concluded that how my uncle talked to me had nothing to do with me. It had nothing to do with my self-worth, whether I was good enough, or who I was. Instead, I realized that how he talked to me had everything to do with who he was, what he was going through, and how he chose to interact with people in his life.

Years of sitting in the circle of men had helped me see that how one individual treated another person had almost nothing to do with the second person. Instead, it had everything to do with that first person. That's because there are many ways for someone to respond to others. Thus, the way they choose to respond says much more about the person responding than about the person being responded to.

That realization improved everything. I didn't need to get angry. I didn't need to feel oppressed. I didn't need to repeatedly tell my uncle how wrong he was for talking to me like that. I'd just be present. I'd still choose to speak my truth. And I'd let him talk however he wanted to talk.

I hadn't been capable of that when I was a kid in his care. Neither had I been capable as an adult until I had sat through the ManKind project's circle of men for a few years. But now I could act from that place. I didn't like it, but I didn't need to get angry or feel bad about myself.

Once I made that shift, a couple of weeks later, I experienced something completely unexpected. One day on a weekend, we got into the car to visit an area he wanted me to see. His partner would be driving the vehicle. I had expected my uncle to take the passenger front seat. However, he offered to sit in the back so I could sit in the front. That way I could have a better view of the countryside. I declined as I wanted to sit in the back. I had planned on writing on the way over. However, right after that moment, as I sat in the back of the car, I felt that warm feeling of feeling loved. It was the first time in my life that I felt loved by my uncle.

Then, I immediately thought, *"What the hell? Am I experiencing Stockholm Syndrome?"*. Then I wondered, *"How can I feel loved by someone who talks to me so disrespectfully? "*

I pondered that over the next couple of days. I realized that once I had stripped away my uncle's words of any meaning about me and let go of his disrespectful way of talking to me, I could finally see his actions completely untainted by his words.

What I saw was how much he did for me: From the food he made sure was cooked for me and to ensuring I had plenty of supplies. He also dedicated much time and care to organizing and showing me around his new region. This man could choose to do nothing for me. Instead, he did a lot for me while I stayed at his place. I saw how he tried to give me the best possible experience he knew while I was at his place.

It was such a paradox. Judging the way he talked to me as being disrespectful, while seeing his actions to be so incredibly loving.

That accusatory stereotype toward some people being all words and no action? I realized my uncle was the opposite.

It was such a pleasant and profound realization. I hadn't sought my uncle's love. He hadn't changed. But now I could experience it.

When it was time to leave his place and travel back home, I left with the thought, *"Oh my god, my uncle actually loves me."*

Looking back, I could now see that his love had always been there. But I couldn't see it before as the words coming out of his mouth hid that love. But now that I could separate what he said from any meaning about me, I could finally see that love. And I could experience it.

Thus, the journey that started at the NWTA with me metaphorically punching my uncle through the punching bag eventually led to me feeling that love from him for the first time. I needed to do the former so I could experience the latter.

Postscript

I've continued sitting in the circle of men throughout the years since my first meeting, even as I wrote this book. The circle of men and the men within it have continued to help me grow significantly. I consider them an essential part of my support system. Several men I sat in a circle during my first circle meeting back in 2014 were still in the same circle I sat in 2023 when I wrote this part of the book. One of those men, Don, designed the cover of this book.

My Reflection

It was sometimes unpredictable where my growth would take me. It was only looking back that I could pinpoint how doing one thing led to another thing, which led to tremendous growth in this other area. It was only then that I could see how interconnected growth can be.

For example, changing my lifestyle allowed me to stop binge eating carbs to bury my anger, which allowed my anger to surface. Without doing that, I wouldn't have been able to use the

171

circle of men so effectively to deal with so many of my causes of anger.

Dealing with all that anger allowed me to then face my uncle. That, in turn, led to a better relationship with him and other strongly assertive people. I no longer had to deal with these individuals as if I were in a flight or fight mode like a rabid dog. I could now address them as equals. Dealing with all that anger and its projections also helped dissipate it and helped me live a much lighter and more peaceful life. And so, in a roundabout way, dealing with my addiction to carbs had a link to years later feeling loved by my uncle.

That tool I learned to clear my anger was a game changer. That's not to say I didn't get angry sometimes; I did. But when I'd get angry, I could see if I was projecting anything from my past onto the situation. Whether I did or not, I could usually respond much calmer and more decisively. That helped me live more from the heart.

Your Reflection

Have you ever had a group of people who can help you grow, keep you accountable, and support you as you develop into a better version of yourself?

How did that work out? What worked? What didn't?

Doing Inner Work

"Who looks outside, dreams; who looks inside, awakens"

Carl Jung

Chapter 15

Embracing Myself
The Story of My Frenchness

Until the age of eight, I lived in France. I had been born in Paris, not far from the Eiffel Tower. My father was French, and my mother was both French and American. When I was six, we moved from Paris to the Normandy region. It was so green, so peaceful, and so beautiful there. It was like the Shire from the Lord of the Rings movie.

When I was in the first grade, the bigger and taller second graders deemed me worthy of hanging out with them. I ran fast enough to keep up with them when we played around the courtyard. I was the only first grader they accepted.

I also was the co-leader of a group of neighbor kids. The other co-leader was one of my best friends who lived on the opposite side of the neighborhood. The neighborhood kids would frequently gather at my family's home.

When I was about seven, I was hanging out with a group of about seven to eight neighborhood kids in my family's backyard. We were sitting on tree logs, talking amongst ourselves. At one point, we spoke of our desire to give our parents a gift. We appreciated what they did for us and wanted to honor them.

However, we had no money and no ability to work. We started pondering about the house in the field next to my family's home. We never saw anyone go in and out of that house. We figured it was abandoned. Surely, nobody would mind if we went in there. So, why don't we break into the house and take an object to give to our parents?

We thought that was a great idea. So, we walked over to the middle of the field behind my parent's house. Then, we gathered around the front of the house. We picked up stones and threw them at the window until it broke. Then, somehow, we got the front door opened. When it came time to go inside, I felt a little scared. But I went ahead with the others. We each looked around for an object to give to our parents. I proudly found one to give my parents and walked out with it.

Later, the local police came to talk to each of us. The objects were all returned, and we were admonished not to do that again. The house apparently was not abandoned. It belonged to someone who only lived there for part of the year.

That put a dead stop to my burgeoning career as the 7-year-old ringleader of a burglary group of kids. Thankfully, the worst that occurred for me was a simple visit by a couple of police officers. All they did was question me at my home. I managed to stay out of any further trouble.

I enjoyed hanging out with my friends and attending school in Normandy. Generally, I felt happy, joyous, and connected.

America

One day, when I was eight years old, disaster struck. It changed everything. It also put an end to my wonderful and happy childhood. My mother announced to my sister and me, "Your father and I are divorcing. I will live in America, and you two are coming with me. "

The only thing I knew about America was that it was far away and was where my grandparents on my mom's side lived. The only time I had ever been to America had been the previous Christmas. We had visited my grandparents on the coast of Georgia. The people in America spoke a weird language. The customs were strange as well.

My sister and I didn't believe people spoke any language other than French. We figured those people in America were talking gibberish. So, we practiced speaking gibberish as well. Then, we would whisper in French to each other what we really meant each time. Surely, we reassured each other that French was the universal language everyone spoke. Even if they sometimes pretended to talk gibberish.

Soon after my mom's announcement, we flew to this strange foreign land. We settled on the coast of Georgia near my grandparents. It was the middle of the summer. It was hot and humid, so different from Normandy's cool weather.

I dreaded the first day of school in America. I tried to will myself to be sick so I wouldn't have to go to school. When I wasn't sick, I tried to pretend to be ill. That didn't work, and we had to go to school.

I thus started my first day of 3rd grade. I didn't speak English, so I was assigned a translator who spoke English and French. She explained how the school system was organized, where, and what I was supposed to do.

I found it odd that students sat alone and isolated at their desks in the classroom. In France, I'd sit with my friends on extended tables. I liked that better. I was also used to staying in the same classroom all day. Now I had to switch classrooms every hour all the time?

The translator was there only for the first day to explain everything to me and translate what the teachers were saying. Starting the second day, I was to follow a fellow third-grade student. They had given us the same classes all day. He knew where we needed to go. He didn't speak French, and I didn't speak English. Nobody else spoke French in that school except my sister, who was in first grade.

So I was now in a strange foreign environment, didn't speak the language, and was in a hot and humid place without any of my friends and without part of my family.

It was hard.

My sister adapted much faster than I did. She learned the language very quickly while I struggled with it. She made friends much quicker, while I also struggled with that.

We spent the summer in France with my French family at the end of the first school year. While in Normandy, my best friend, whom I had sent letters to during the year, basically didn't care to spend much time with me. He had moved on.

Back in America, I did make one friend in elementary school. But I went to a different middle school, and that friendship dissipated. In middle school, I only had one friend. Then, he and I got into a fistfight in eighth grade, and the friendship ended.

After living in America for a few years, when my father visited us one day, he asked me, "What nationality are you?" I said, "I don't know". He said, "You are French! Remember that! Don't forget you are French!"

However, I wanted to forget. I was starting to admire America. I loved learning the country's history and how the American Revolution shaped the freedoms enjoyed in America. I also saw how there was so much more abundance than there was in France. People could buy more gaming systems than in France for the same amount. That was an important consideration for a boy my age.

However, I was having trouble fitting in. I struggled with that. In France, I had many friends and was a leader. In America, I barely had one friend at a time. It seemed to me that my trouble with fitting in America came from the part of me that was different. The part of me that was French.

So, slowly, I started repressing that French side of me. Trying to forget I was French. However, my French accent would come out whenever I spoke English. This was unlike my sister, who spoke English flawlessly without an accent.

I started to hate hearing people speak with an accent. It reminded me of my accent. I'd fly with my sister each summer to stay with my French family. As soon as we'd land in Paris, I'd dislike hearing the French language. The language felt cold and harsh. I loved listening to the sweet, comforting sound of English when I returned to the US Airport after my three-month stay in France.

In 11th grade, I wrote an essay for a school contest called "Why I'm Proud to Be an American." I won first place in my grade level and received a cash prize. I was also invited to read my essay at a local veteran's group. I wasn't a US citizen yet.

Eventually, I became so rusty in French that I had difficulty reading in French. The language started to feel like a foreign language. France became a foreign country to me.

But I still didn't fit in in America. I had few friends in high school. I also had several fistfights with local rural boys who didn't like me.

When I turned 18, I immediately applied for US Citizenship. Once I got my citizenship, I immediately wrote to the French Embassy to renounce my French citizenship. There was then a peacetime draft in France. I thought the only way to avoid being drafted into the French military was to renounce my citizenship. At the time, I didn't mind losing my French citizenship.

The French Embassy wrote back that it was impossible to renounce my French citizenship. However, since I was living overseas, I would be excluded from the peacetime military draft.

Soon after receiving my US Citizenship, I went off to college. I was introduced to the Internet during my first few weeks in college. A classmate introduced me to an online 2D tank game. In the game, we'd drive this little tank and shoot other players as we tried to capture bases. It was a lot of fun. There was an online community around this game, mostly college students nationwide.

We communicated by writing messages during the game, as this was way before the advent of widespread Internet voice chat. We'd type fast and furiously to our allies. The faster we typed, the better we could coordinate tactics and strategy. In between games, we'd hang out casually in the chat rooms and write messages in the group chat. We'd also write posts in the newsgroup dedicated to the game.

For the first time, I could communicate with people without my accent coming through. Nobody could tell that I was a "foreigner" and not "American" like the others. For the first time since I landed in America, I felt like I fit into a community. It was an online gaming community, but it was a community nevertheless. I started spending a lot of time on it.

Years later, I realized how toxic of a community it was. I eventually decided that if I was going to have any hope of fixing my dysfunctional life, I needed to walk away from that community. So, I left.

Embracing my Frenchness

When I was in my early 30s and living in Las Vegas, I went through graduate school. I attended a series of personal development workshops. My good friend Boniebelle, who was also attending one of those workshops with me, was starting to give intuitive readings. One evening, she gave me such a reading.

During the reading, she said, "You need to embrace that French side of you fully. You've been repressing it for so long, and yet there is so much good in that side of you.".

I felt as if I was struck by a lightning bolt. That was the first time I heard the idea of embracing the French side of me. That felt strange to consider. But I also immediately knew she was right. I had tried to deny, repress, and suppress the French side of me for almost two decades.

What would happen if I did embrace my Frenchness? Would I end up getting rejected even more? Would I be shunned? I had operated under that assumption. I now realized maybe I was wrong.

I wrote in my journal:

> *"Frenchness: let go of negative aspect. Change to positive. Let go of it feels wrong. Accept it and embrace it.*

Frenchness; I think people judge me. We are different in so many ways. I wish I didn't feel so different, but that's where my best part lies.

Time to appreciate my differences as beautiful and not shun them...What I think is wrong actually inspires others. Develop deep appreciation, reach for feeling, and let go.

How [can I] appreciate [my] Frenchness?

What aspect of Frenchness am I proud of?"

I knew what it was like to repress my Frenchness. But I didn't know what it was like to embrace it. So, I decided to embrace my Frenchness with open arms fully. I was curious to see what would happen.

I pondered, *"How could I do that?"*

First, I decided to change how I pronounced my name. I had let English speakers determine how to pronounce my name when I came to America. I'd introduce my first and last name, the "American way." I also had gotten to hate my name. I hadn't linked the two together until much later.

This showed up when I worked in retail stores in my 20s. I'd usually wear a different name badge than my own. I also sometimes wondered about changing my first name permanently to a different one. But I never found another name I liked enough.

But now, having decided to embrace my Frenchness fully, I decided to pronounce my full name in French. The way it was given to me at birth. No longer would I use the bastardized English manner of saying my name.

So, the next day at the workshop, as soon as I walked in, I told one of the organizers the "new" way to pronounce my name. Hearing her say it back sounded so sweet to me. I started then to tell everyone I knew, my friends and family.

I also started to use the French pronunciation whenever I met someone new. I felt like a new person when I did that. I loved it.

I noticed that after all of these years of disliking my name, I started to love my name again. The problem all along wasn't that I disliked my name but that I had disliked the English way of pronouncing it.

Next, I started to read in French again. I also reviewed what I was ashamed of in French history. I devised a way to respond to how people have teased me about some aspects—by embracing them. I also put the French flag on my wall at home.

Five months later, I visited my family in France for a month. For the first time in many years, the French language at the Paris airport sounded sweet and welcoming. France didn't feel like a foreign country anymore. Instead, it now felt like my country.

Back in the US, I eventually moved to Dallas, Texas, and started to join local communities.

While I needed to do some inner work (see "Diffusing Triggers: The Tale of Button Love") to join these communities, I felt so welcomed once in. Despite being the only French man there and fully embracing my Frenchness, I felt I fit in. I felt accepted for who I was. I noticed that I wasn't being teased anymore about that aspect of French history that I used to be teased. I ended up experiencing a wonderful social life in Dallas, where I fit in more than ever.

My Reflection

Growing up, I thought I needed to repress my French side to fit in. But I was so wrong. Only when I fully embraced myself and the French side did I eventually find that I fit in.

Fully embracing the French side didn't mean repressing the American side of me. I also fully embrace that American side of me. I'm not half French and half American. I consider myself 100% French and 100% American.

There are so many ways that we sometimes are made to feel that we need to repress a side of us to fit in. Sometimes that pressure may be external, and sometimes it may be internal. Sometimes, it's not as apparent as national origins. It can be a quirk in our personality. Or it can be an interest that we have. Or it can be an experience we like having.

When I tried to hide aspects of myself, those who would appreciate those parts of me had a hard time finding me. Instead, I would mostly be with people who couldn't appreciate all of me. I've learned that the more I could embrace all aspects of myself, then the more other people also embraced and accepted all of me. It may not be the same people – some people who didn't accept that part of me may have gone away. That worked out because then those people who appreciated that part of me would finally be able to find me and come into my life.

In addition, I knew that the more I fully embraced myself, the more I gave others permission to embrace themselves, and that helped everyone live more from the heart.

Your Reflection

What part of you are ashamed of or afraid others will judge you? What part of yourself are you repressing, suppressing, and hoping no one finds out?

What can you do to start to love and embrace that part of yourself?

(Note: If the part of yourself you are repressing was involved in acts that would be dangerous or illegal, then perhaps ask yourself, "How can I accept my past while knowing that I will never commit those actions again?")

Chapter 16

Uncovering and Changing Hidden Beliefs
The Story of the Four Women

After Josephine broke up with me in 2008, I decided to do my best to live from the heart. That resulted in a tremendous amount of growth as I faced many fears.

However, there was a darker side effect from the aftermath of dating Josephine. It took me two years to realize it. While working hard to live more from the heart, I was betraying one of my important values in one domain.

About six months after the breakup, I rented a room in a home in a new city. The hosts were a married couple who were a little younger than me. I enjoyed hanging out with both of them.

Once in a while I would hang out with the wife while the husband was at work. She desired to be a mother more than anything else. We had a lot of fun talking with each other. It was innocent. Until it wasn't. One evening, while we were hanging out late, she leaned in to kiss me. I wasn't expecting that. I wasn't trying to make anything happen. However, on a subconscious level, perhaps I wasn't surprised. There had been an undercurrent of energy running between us.

It wasn't the first time an attractive married woman tried to kiss me. I had stopped a previous attempt from another attractive married woman. I had stopped her out of principle that I didn't kiss married women. It wouldn't be fair to her husband.

But this time, I didn't stop it. I didn't resist it.

And so we kissed. Soon after, we did more than kiss.

There was no discussion regarding a relationship between us. There was no romance either between us. She was just cheating on her husband with me. I guess we were both going through a hard time in life. We found some comfort in each other. We had to hide my involvement with her from her husband.

I wasn't aware that a new pattern had started in my life.

Not long afterward, I sat outside, observing the couple while they talked and interacted. I felt incredibly guilty about what I was doing to her husband. I didn't like it.

I soon became uncomfortable with the whole living situation. I moved to another place and stopped hanging out with either of them.

Next, I spent a lot of time with an international student from a Middle East Muslim-ruled country. She was a studious woman who worked hard in school. She told me she was single. When I first met her, I found her ugly. I had no interest in dating her. But after spending much time together, I started seeing her differently. We both began to develop feelings for each other. As a result, we became involved with each other.

However, she was forbidden from her country's religion and culture to date Westerners. If one of her local friends saw us together, they'd report her to family back home. She would then face substantial problems. Thus, we hid our involvement from everyone who knew both of us. We were also careful not to be caught publicly. Despite being careful publicly, she did get a thrill sneaking kisses while we were outside and secluded. It was forbidden in her country to kiss outside.

Nevertheless, my new pattern continued with someone new. I still hadn't noticed it.

After things fizzled out with the Muslim woman, I became involved with a woman in her mid-20's. She was a nerd working in a technical field. I had met her online, although we had many mutual friends.

She had never dated anyone and held firmly to her identity of "I don't date people." When we started dating, she didn't want any of our mutual friends to know about us. It would go against her identity of being someone who didn't date. I honored her request. We spent about seven months being involved with each other while hiding it from our mutual friends.

And so my new pattern continued while I was utterly oblivious to it.

Then, I met another woman online with whom I became close friends She was a highly elegant woman who was also a bit of a nomad and lived far away. Eventually, I developed an attraction toward her. She visited the city I lived in and stayed in town for an extended time. My attraction toward her felt even stronger when we met in person. I told her I wanted to kiss her. We ended up getting involved with each other.

However, she had a husband back home. I had been aware of that the whole time. So, we had to hide our involvement from our mutual friends. We also hid it from social media so her husband would not find out.

And so my new pattern was continuing with a new person. I was completely blind to it.

Thankfully, though, this latest woman could see what was happening. She realized what she was doing was wrong. She decided to come clean with her husband.

She also asked me, "What is going on with you? What is your karma in all that you are doing? Why do you keep getting involved with all of us women who have to hide you?"

That's when it hit me like a tsunami. That's when I realized for the first time that for the last two years, each woman I was involved with had to hide me for one reason or another. It wasn't like that before. But now it was. If it had happened only once, that'd be one thing. But this was a pattern repeating itself. And the common thread in all of this was me.

What craziness was going on within me? Why was I betraying my values? Why did I attract different kinds of women who had nothing in common with each other except the need to hide me and my involvement with them?

Inner Work

Three years earlier, I had found the wisdom of journaling regularly. By writing my thoughts down, I significantly improved the process of examining my thoughts and seeing what they were. Keeping things in my head keeps things scrambled. Writing it down helped to clarify things significantly and helped me grow much better.

Thus, later that day, I opened up my journal. I wrote:

"am going to do[guided] meditation on why I attract relationships where I have to hide it. Why? [She] had a good point about not hiding our love for each other, and how it

wasn't [the] path to truth...she said it felt shameful for her to hide it. I agree. I don't resonate with hiding it at all and prefer it being in the open."

I put on a guided meditation to access my subconscious to get answers. After it was over, I wrote in my journal:

"The reason is that I felt it was wrong for me to be involved in a relationship - because I couldn't keep up what I had said. I had gotten into extreme pain after the breakup with Josephine, the worst pain ever. I remember it was so horrible...the pain was so overwhelming...Then I cried for six weeks and felt hurt for a long time.
I felt I had lived a lie. All along, I had said, "No big deal if we break up. I can handle it." I could handle it beforehand, but I couldn't with Josephine. I felt it was wrong to be in a relationship if I couldn't handle the breakup...especially since I claimed I could handle it."

I kept journaling to explore the situation. The next day, I wrote:

"[The new belief I formed was] I'm not worthy of having a relationship, and thus it's wrong for me to have one.". Hence... I attracted women who themselves felt it was wrong to be involved with me and, thus, not willing to be open about it. "

That was such a lightbulb moment for me. I could now so clearly see how the intense pain of breaking up with Josephine led me to believe I was not worthy of relationships. I then attracted women who also believed that about me. And that led me to, in part, break my principle of not being involved with married women cheating on their husbands.

Thus, I concluded that the way out of this was to change the belief that I wasn't worthy of relationships.

I wasn't sure how to go about it. So, I figured I'd start by laying some ground rules. First, no more dating anyone who must hide me. If a woman needs to hide me and our involvement from people who know both of us, then that will be a red flag to moving forward. Second, no more getting involved with any married woman at all. Unless her husband was completely okay with it and they were in an ethical, non-monogamy relationship.

Then, I figured I needed to replace the belief of "I am not worthy of being in a relationship" with something more empowering. I decided to return to my previous belief that "I am worthy of relationships."

So, I first remembered how I used to believe I was worthy of such relationships. I thought of the women I had dated openly before without hiding. I then forgave myself for hurting so long after Josephine. I also forgave myself for being wrong and thinking I could get over her quickly. Finally, I started reinforcing the belief that I was worthy of a relationship.

I was going through a lot wrapping up graduate school before moving on, so I didn't do much in terms of dating. However, several months later, I noticed I had deepened my friendship with a married woman I had known for a few years. I also noticed I felt attracted to her. And that she seemed attracted to me as well. I was starting to feel that now-familiar sense of exciting energy building up between us. However, she was in a monogamous relationship. Thus, if I got involved with her, I'd be breaking my value of honoring other people's marriages. And I'd need to hide again.

I felt like the universe was testing me. It was as if the universe told me, "Are you serious about being worthy of a relationship? About never getting involved with a married woman who would need to cheat on her husband to be with you? Here's another tempting, attractive married woman for you. Here's your test to see if you were serious about your decision".

It would be easy to continue my pattern, but where would that get me? Where would betraying my values get me? Who would I become?

Soon after, in a conversation with my married friend, I talked with her about how I don't get involved with married women. After that conversation, things did seem to cool off between us. We stayed on as friends, but we never got involved.

I felt I had passed the test from the universe.

Not long afterward, through friends, I met a woman. She was single, and we started dating. Our friends knew we were dating, and I didn't have to hide anything! What a fresh breath of air!

Later, I dated another woman. She posted a picture of us two on social media right after our first date. She declared to her many followers that she was now dating me. I was taken aback. I wasn't ready to declare to the world after only one date. I chuckled, though, as I thought that I now have the opposite problem I used to have.

My Reflection

One of the most powerful ways I found to change my behavior, and thus my results, was by changing my beliefs or thoughts underneath that behavior.

One great way I've found to change limiting beliefs is by using Byron Katie's tool, "The Work." I didn't use it here in this story because I had other evidence and memories of my previous life I could refer to, but I have used it in many different situations.

The hardest thing for my growth was becoming aware of a pattern or belief that negatively impacted my life. Once I had discovered what that was, I would get excited. Because now that I could see it, I could change it.

That's because beliefs acted like colored lenses in glasses. The world looked different based on the lenses. And based on how I saw the world or my life, I would act and think accordingly. That then produced specific results that broadly matched the lens. When I changed the lens through which I see the world, I acted differently and thought differently. That then produced different results.

That's not to say changing beliefs was necessarily easy. Sometimes, it took a lot of work. It may have required journaling, inner work, and exploration. It may have required courageous actions in an uncomfortable new area.

Upgrading limiting beliefs was like upgrading a three-legged stool. The seat of the stool acted like the belief, while the legs were the evidence supporting the belief. When I installed a new thought or belief, I liked to gather evidence that it was true and accurate. Perhaps it was even truer and more accurate than the previous belief. The faster I could add new legs to the new seat, the quicker the new belief could be built. This created new results in life, thus reinforcing the new belief even more.

Your Reflection

What is something unfortunate that keeps happening to you repeatedly in life?

If you've identified such a pattern, then these steps may help:

- What is your underlying belief about this or this situation?
- Apply Byron Katie's The Work to your belief.
- How can you reinforce your new belief and build evidence until that belief becomes second nature?

Chapter 17

Transforming Life Completely
The Story of One Hour a Day

In September 2013, five years after deciding to learn to live from the heart, I found myself floundering in my job search and other areas of my life, such as my fitness.

I had by then been unemployed for a couple of years after graduating with my master's degree. I had made a lot of sacrifices to try to live a life from the heart. I had given up a possible lucrative career in the oil industry. I had moved back in with my mother. However, my new career search wasn't working out. It was going nowhere.

Furthermore, I didn't just want to transform my career but also my relationships, friendships, fitness, finances, living situation, community involvement, and so much more. I had made much progress over the past five years, but I wanted to make many more changes.

I was feeling intensely frustrated. I posted on Facebook with the words, "I feel stuck."

What I didn't write in the Facebook post was that my growth seemed to come in spurts. I would intensely focus on my growth for a few days or a week, and then I'd languish for weeks or months. I didn't spend any time on my growth during that languishing time. So, most of my experience in life was feeling stuck.

What I was doing clearly wasn't working. It wasn't completely broken either, though. The times I focused on my growth did work. I could make transformations in some areas once in a while. But at this rate, I would take over 1,000 years to become the man I wanted to be. So, since humans generally don't live beyond 100 years, it would be impossible.

How could I grow much faster and experience many more transformations? How can I transform not just one area of my life, my career, but all areas? How can I not be so lazy for so long regarding my growth?

While contemplating this, I felt this sense within me that I needed to change my approach to growth. I needed to stop waiting until I was either, on the one hand, inspired or, on the other hand, in pain. Instead, I needed continuous daily momentum. Maybe that would be the key?

I reasoned it out. Some say we can grow 1% a day. However, an entire life encompasses so much. It includes health, career, emotions, relationships, spirituality, friendships, finances, households, etc. It seemed too much to change 1% of it in one day. Ok, so that is out.

But what about improving my life by 1/10th of 1%? Somehow, that seemed more doable as that appeared to be a tiny number.

If I improved my life by one-tenth of one percent each day after 30 days, that is a little over three percent compounded. That's not much of a change. However, compoundly, after a year of daily one tenth of one percent growth, that would add up to 44%. That starts to be significant. If I extrapolate it to five years, that would add up to 519% with compound growth. Now, that's huge.

Maybe life transforming. Thus, daily the increase wouldn't be perceptible, but it could be ultimately revolutionizing in the long term.

OK, I liked that a lot. But what would my growth look like?

Looking back, I realized I had tried to change so much of what was around me for years by working directly on those things. If I didn't like my relationships, I'd try to change those relationships. If I didn't like where I lived, I'd complain about where I lived and try to force a change.

Sometimes, that would work in the short term. However, the same situation would come up repeatedly in the long term. Instead, what worked better was when I dealt with making changes within myself as I made changes on the outside. It created much more durable and successful changes.

I reasoned then that my results were primarily dependent on my actions. My actions were then dependent on my thoughts. Thus, at the simplest level, if I wanted to change my results for good, I needed to change my thoughts.

But first, I would need to know what my thoughts were. That also meant knowing what my beliefs and emotions were. It meant having a better understanding of what was going on within me. One way I could do that on my own would be through journaling and guided meditation. I could then work on changing those thoughts through one tool or another. I decided to call that "inner work."

That's as opposed to doing what I decided to call "outer work," which is consuming growth material such as audiobooks, podcasts, books, etc. I still thought it had a place in my life to serve as inspiration and information on how I could grow.

I decided to spend half of my growth time on my "inner work" and half on "outer work."

Ok, so if I need to spend time on this daily for continuous growth, how much time would it take?

The answer that was coming to me was one full hour a day. At first, that seemed huge. Would I even have the discipline? Or would I be too lazy for that? What about the time when I'm super busy? What about when I was in a bad mood all day?

I thought about it. I reasoned that one hour a day equals seven hours a week. There are 168 hours a week, so seven hours only equals 4.2% of my time. I would still have 95.8% of my time to do other things. So, looking at it from that perspective, spending 4.2% of my time on my growth didn't seem much.

How could I overcome laziness by spending an hour on my daily growth?

For that, I decided to use two psychological tools: First, I decided to try doing a 30-day trial where I'd spend one hour a day for 30 days. Second, I decided to make this the most important thing I'd do for the next 30 days. That way, I wouldn't have any excuse not to do this.

I felt I had a lot hanging on this.

30 Day Trial

Thus, on October 4th, 2013, I started my 30-day trial of spending one hour daily on my growth. I wanted to see if I could do this and what the effects might be.

Early on, I decided I didn't need to spend the whole hour at once. I could spend 5 minutes here, 20 minutes there, 12 minutes later, etc. Every time I'd work on my growth, I'd set my phone's stopwatch until I completed that session.

Then, each time I was finishing a session, I'd mark how much time I spent on a note on my phone. I kept track of my time until I hit one hour for the day, and then I'd stop monitoring it. My goal would be to hit one hour each day by the time I fell asleep that night.

I also realized I didn't need to be in front of my computer. If I were somewhere outside the home, I could use my phone's note system to journal my thoughts and emotions as I worked through them.

One day, I was in a bad mood and feeling incredibly lazy. I stayed up late watching some movies. It was about 3 am when I stopped. I then realized I still had 45 minutes to finish my growth hour. I was feeling so tired, and the temptation was there to go to sleep. But no, I told myself I made a deal to do this for 30 days. To grow a little bit each day. So, I pulled up my journal and journaled until I finished my inner work. Then, I pulled a nonfiction book on my Kindle and forced myself to stay awake to read it to finish my outer work. My eyes closed briefly, but as soon as they did, I reopened my eyes to finish reading until I had done my one hour. When I went to bed, I felt satisfied that I had done a little bit of growth that day.

I felt a sense of accomplishment each day as I finished my hour. I was still far from having the life I wanted. But I was moving forward at least a bit by doing that one hour.

After thirty days, I evaluated my trial. I didn't see much transformation in my life. But then one-tenth of one percent daily for a month is only slightly over three percent compounded. That's barely perceptible, if at all. But I did experience one change: I didn't feel stuck anymore. I was moving forward. I knew that as long as I spent that one hour a day on my growth, I could have hope for a much better future. Thus, I decided to continue.

Continuing the Hour

I attended a board game convention in Dallas a month and a half after starting my daily hour. How could I spend an hour daily on my growth while playing board games? By then, though, I was hooked. I would take breaks between games to go outside. I'd then spend my time on my growth until it eventually totaled an hour each day.

Thanksgiving came, and I spent one hour on my growth that day. Christmas, New Year's Eve, and New Year's Day came and went. I spent an hour on my growth each of those days and all the days in between. Same later with my birthday.

Soon, within a few months, I was able to transform my inability to run into being able to run 5 K's! That was thanks to spending that hour a day on my growth. The inner work helped the most successfully tackle that problem.

By then, I was experiencing on a daily basis how much more powerful my inner work was than my outer work. Thus, I decided to lift my requirement to spend half of my growth time on outside work. Therefore, I started to allow myself to spend the entire daily hour on inner work if I so chose to.

At one point, I caught an illness and was sick in bed for most of the day. I only had a few hours of consciousness each day for a few days. I still made sure I spent one of those hours on my growth. By now, nothing would deter me from spending time on my development. I knew this hour was the key to transforming my life. I knew I had hope for a better future as long as I did this.

Ten years

In the next ten years, I only missed doing the full hour half a dozen times. Each time, I went to sleep thinking I had finished the hour when I hadn't. I realized I hadn't finished that hour each time I woke up the following day. So, I would finish the previous day's hour before doing anything else. I'd do that even before getting out of bed. Then I started that day's hour.

Within ten years of starting this habit, I completed a sprint Triathlon and competed in 60+ races, including two half marathons.

I got rid of 400+ triggers so that I could start showing up to social events without massive anxiety. I also learned to deal with anger effectively through ManKind project. All of that revolutionized my social life, as well as my dating life and friendships. This led to also becoming much more integrated into local communities.

I landed my dream job two years after starting this habit. Then, I eventually transformed my work to be remote, fulfilling a long-time dream.

I started traveling worldwide, visiting places I had always dreamed of visiting in Asia and Europe.

I created so many powerful habits for myself, including meditation, gratitude practice, morning and evening routines that anchored my life, and so much more.

I learned to live from the heart so much better. My life is night and day compared to how it used to be.

And so much more. My relationships, friendships, spirituality, finances, and household situations have all been powerfully transformed. My ability to contribute to the world and impact has also massively increased.

No area of my life has been untouched by my growth. I've become far more capable than I used to be regarding my skill sets. I've also become far more capable of experiencing life to its fullest. All thanks to that one hour a day, every single day, no matter what.

That's not to say life is always perfect. It's not. I don't expect it to be. I've still had plenty of times where I experienced frustration. I've still had bad days. Sometimes, I might experience setbacks in one area. For example, I experienced a heartbreaking relationship breakup that took me a long time to get over. Later, I experienced an injury that kept me from running for over a year. However, if one area of my life might take a temporary backslide, I'm still growing in other areas. Thus, I haven't felt stuck in life since I started this habit. Instead, I've experienced continuous growth.

That calculation I made before starting where I figured that if I grow one-tenth of one percent a day, compounded, it'd add up to 519% in five years. It came out to be true. It's no longer going to take 1,000 years for me to transform. I can do it fast enough to enjoy the results in this lifetime.

Looking back on the ten years since I started this habit, every year has been measurably better than the previous year. Even during the years of the pandemic. Sure, maybe not every single area of my life. But overall, each year has been better than before. I attribute that to the never-ending growth.

That makes getting older exciting. Each year I get older is another year I've spent on my growth. It's another year in which I expand my capabilities and ability to experience life at an expanded level. It's another year of living more into my vision of what could be. And it's another year of learning to live more from the heart.

But more than the results, I have adored spending that hour (or more) daily on my growth. It feels very nourishing. It's fun. Knowing I'm creating something new in my life is exciting and joyous. I feel fulfilled spending that time on my growth.

And so, one day will be my last day on Earth. Hopefully, I'll be a very old man. I like to think that on that last day, I'll still do my hour of growth before I take my last breath.

My Reflection

Daily growth made life transformation happen much faster than it would otherwise have. The daily changes may not be perceptible, but they were significant in the long run.

Inner work has been remarkable in allowing me to show up more as the person I wanted to be. It's been a crucial part of learning to live more from the heart.

However, I found that spending daily time on my growth was crucial not only for my development but also for dealing with all that life throws at me.

Was something bothering me? Inner work. Being laid off? Dealing with a breakup? Physical injury? All dealt with inner work, followed by action. My boss angry at me? I'm angry at my boss? Relationship troubles? All dealt with inner work.

Like dust piles up inside a home, I knew my brain could gather the "dust" of all these issues. However, doing the inner work kept my brain clean, like a vacuum machine keeps a home clean. It prevented these things from sticking to me and dragging me down, keeping life exciting and fresh.

I also knew there was no standing still in life. I was either growing, or I was regressing. Too much in life came at me for me to be able to stand still. I might think I would be standing still if I tried. But I'd actually be regressing. I saw that in my 20's, after college, when my circle of life became smaller and smaller. If I had kept on that path, I might have become a bitter and angry person like I've seen many become. That would have kept me further away from living from the heart.

How did I learn to live more from the heart? By doing the daily inner work. The rest were details.

Your Reflection

Looking back at the last ten years of your life:

How did you successfully transform areas of your life over time?

What areas of your life have progressed?

What areas have gotten worse?

Over the next ten years, what areas of life would you most like to improve?

Chapter 18

Releasing Shame
The Story of Interviewing

In 2014, I was at a standstill with my job search. I had been unemployed for a few years. I wanted to land a job I could do from the heart. Thus, I sought out help.

As a result, I started attending workshops on landing such a job. These were twelve-week workshops covering different aspects of the job search, such as resume writing, networking, interviewing, and much more.

One day, a helpful volunteer asked me, "What is your work history?"

I wanted to yell, "None of your business!".

But I didn't. Instead, my body stiffened while I mumbled something. I didn't want to reveal my work history. It seemed like it would be a bad thing to do. The volunteer left my table to talk to someone who was probably more receptive.

I continued attending these workshops. Whenever someone would try to help me by asking what skill sets I had or inquiring about my work history, I would shut down again. I didn't know why, but it seemed like revealing my work history would be dangerous.

After the third or fourth time of being asked, I journaled about it:

"How am I going to be able to sit in a job interview when I know they'll want to talk about my past? They will notice how cagey and resistant I am to that discussion, and the interview will end with me getting no job.
Why am I so cagey?
Why do I don't want to talk about my work history?"

At first, I didn't know. It just seemed natural to me to react this way. I had been that way for a long time.

I probed. I let the answer surface. Then it hit me:

"I am ashamed of my work history."

Growing up, I had been told the importance of sticking to one job/one career. I had already switched between four careers in four industries by my mid-30s. And I didn't want to go back to any of these. Instead, I wanted to do something different that spoke more to my heart. I didn't know what that might be.

Thus, I feared people would judge me to be inconsistent and unreliable. And therefore, they wouldn't want to help me get a job. Or they wouldn't want to hire me. Or that they'd ridicule me for even thinking that maybe I could work in a job, I'd love given my shameful work history.

That felt very heavy to me.

What could I do? If I spoke about my job history, I would risk being rejected and told how bad I am for having switched around so much. I might also feel a lot of shame. The alternative was to keep my job history hidden and react cagey. However, an essential part of a job interview is discussing the candidate's job history. How could I interview if I couldn't talk about my job history? I'd end up getting rejected.

I didn't know what to do. So, I decided to dive deep into exploring what shame was.

Shame

As I researched online about shame, I read through a paper written in the 90's. That paper explored the topic of shame concerning an individual's sexual orientation. The paper explained how hiding a person's sexuality (such as in the case of homosexuality) led to the individual feeling ashamed. Then, the sense of shame led them to hide it more. It was a vicious spiraling down cycle. The act of hiding led to feeling more shame. Then, the feeling of shame led to more hiding.

The research paper said that to stop feeling shameful, that which brings shame must be talked with other people. When people share or talk about what they consider shameful in their lives, it is like they are stopping the cycle of hiding. That then reduces the feeling of shame. And when people feel less shame, they have less of a need to hide it. Thus, they then talk more about it, creating an upward cycle.

The paper discussed how the pride parade organizers designed it to help remove the shame individuals felt around their sexuality. By being seen and accepted openly by others, their shame would decrease. Eventually, what used to bring shame can instead bring on a sense of pride if this process continues.

Given how far along the gay rights movement had come since the 90s when the paper was written, it seemed that the pride parades had been effective.

I correlated that with other resources. It seemed straightforward: The best way to get rid of feelings of shame is to share with others exactly what I feel shameful about.

Healing Shame

There was no pride parade for job history, so I thought, "*What can I do? What if I started talking to people about my job history? Would that help alleviate my feelings of shame? But what if people rejected me when I mentioned my job history? What if it made things worse and made it harder to get a job?*"

I knew where being ashamed of my job history got me: I didn't get interviews. I couldn't be assisted by people who knew much more about landing jobs than I did. That path seemed clear, and it led to nowhere.

So, I figured, let's try the other path. The path of lessening my shame regarding my job history by not hiding it anymore. The only thing I didn't know was how people would respond.

The shame felt heavy in me, so I thought I'd start with the easiest audience: My mom. One evening, while we were relaxing, I said, "Mom, I want to talk about my job history.". My mom knew my job history, but I wanted to discuss it and how I felt shameful about it. It was a way to stop hiding the shame and start to put it out there.

While talking, I felt sensitive and tender. My mom listened to me. And she didn't reject me for having brought that up. I felt better by the end. I had let a little light shine in.

Having had one discussion in which I discussed the shame, I then called up my close friend Steve. Steve and I had known each other for over 15 years. I relied on him as part of my support group. I started the same conversation as I did with my mom. Explained the shame I felt about my job history. It was a little easier this time around. He listened and didn't reject me either. I felt a little better afterward.

Ok, so I had talked to the two closest people in my life. They accepted me. But would others accept me or reject me?

I also knew I couldn't just attend the workshops and talk to the volunteers. That was too hard. Too risky. Too big of a jump.

So, I called one of my local friends on the phone. She had only known me for a few years and knew little about my job history. I had kept it hidden since I felt ashamed of it. But on the phone, I slowly described to her the different careers and industries I worked in. She listened as well and was supportive. I felt glad I had shared it when I got off the phone. I was letting more light into that part of me that felt shameful.

I continued and initiated conversations about my job history with about 3-4 more local friends. That happened either on the phone or in person. They all were recent friends, so they didn't know much about my past.

Each person I shared with made it easier to tell the next person about my work history. With each conversation, I felt less shameful. A heavy weight was slowly lifted off me, one conversation at a time.

After these conversations, I wondered what was next. I still couldn't bring it up in a workshop. While the weight had diminished from talking with my friends, it still felt too heavy.

I then thought, Let's share it on social media! So, I wrote a post on Facebook and started with, "In the last 15 years, I've had four major careers in four industries.". In the post, I listed my careers and how I was looking to start my fifth career.

I felt a lot of anxiety before I hit the "post" button. I posted the post and walked away. I didn't want to check what anyone had written in my post for the rest of the day. I thought it might be painful to read.

Much later in the day, I opened up Facebook. I braced myself for what I might read. As I read through the comments, I saw so many that were so supportive! Instead of the pain I feared I might feel, I felt so touched.

One of my friends even wrote about how I was a "Renaissance Man" like he was for working in various fields. For the first time, I had an inkling that there might be a benefit to switching careers. Perhaps it wasn't all bad?

After posting on Facebook and experiencing the result, I noticed how I felt a lot less ashamed about my job history. I had shined a lot of light on what had been a dark place in me. I was spiraling upward.

I finally felt ready to return to the job search workshops and talk to volunteers about it. When I spoke to the first volunteer about my job history, they gave me good feedback about how I can use that to land a job I'd love! I experienced acceptance instead of the rejection and condemnation I feared.

Some volunteers talked to me about how my job history showed adaptability, broad experiences, and a unique perspective that I could bring to a new job. They also explained to me how I had a wide variety of skill sets that I could bring to any job.

I thought, *"Wow, I didn't even think about that."*

When I was ashamed of my job history, all I could think about was how it showed that I was unreliable and inconsistent. But now I had confronted my shame by sharing it. As a result, I discovered that my job history showed many positive qualities about myself. These are qualities that an employer would love to have in an employee.

After talking with several volunteers, my shame was utterly gone. I could now talk about my job history with ease. I started to join networking groups and easily talked about my background. As a result, people gave me even more helpful advice and support about landing the kind of job I wanted.

One day, after a long search, I was finally sitting before two hiring managers. They were interviewing me for my dream job. I wanted this job more than any other job I ever had applied for. It was for a job I had never done in an industry I had never worked in. As the hiring manager asked me about my background, I proudly discussed how specific aspects of the different careers in my past had prepared me well to take on the job they were hiring for.

They liked what I had to say and how I said it, and more specifically, they liked my work history.

I was hired.

My shame had turned into pride. Just like the research paper said, it would.

My Reflection

Shame and its cousin guilt wanted to make me hide in fear of judgment from others. It wanted to make me afraid that others may find something out about me that I judged myself negatively. It was pretty insidious. That's no way to live from the heart.

Sometimes, some negative consequences of disclosing things we were ashamed of may be loss of jobs, relationships, or family ties. I know that in my case, if a job, a relationship, or family ties required me to feel shame and guilt, then it was not worth it. It means I wouldn't be accepted for who I am. I'd rather spend my time and energy where I was accepted as I am.

When I shared what I had been afraid of sharing, I felt such freedom and a lifting of the weight on me. Many times, when I've shared things I feared being judged for, my fears were overblown. Instead, I attracted more people who loved that part of me and accepted me as I am. They accepted me in a way that wouldn't have been possible before when I kept things much more hidden.

I do know we need to be careful in sharing with people who may be physically violent toward us as a result. However, when there is no immediate threat of physical violence, there are ways to deal with any potential negative consequences. The positive results of overcoming shame made it worthwhile for me. It also helped me live more from the heart.

Your Reflection

What things have you done that you're afraid other people will discover about you?

If you feel any shame or guilt, ask yourself: Who can you start sharing this with to begin your journey to transform the feelings of shame or guilt into something better?

Chapter 19

Listening to My Inner Voice
The Story of Landing My Dream Job

The year after I decided to align with love, I asked myself, how can I live from the heart if I can't hear my heart?

That became apparent when I talked to my online friend Camila. I had asked her how I could develop my intuition. I figured that would help me receive guidance from the universe to help me live from the heart.

Camila started asking me questions to see what my subconscious was telling me. As I tried to answer her, I'd stumble. I'd say one thing. Then I'd say, "No, that's not it". I'd then blurt out something else instead. I couldn't make up my mind about what my subconscious was telling me.

She then kindly told me I needed to be able to discern and trust what my subconscious told me. Otherwise, I'd have no hope of developing my intuition. And I realized that I could not listen well to my heart either.

My dilemma was that I didn't trust most of the signals within me.

Growing up, the messages I received from the adults constantly reinforced the notion that what I wanted and what I was thinking couldn't be trusted. That it was likely not the right way to do things.

Then, in my early 20s, I dived deep into Tony Robbin's workshops and learned about NLP. A significant portion of what I learned about NLP is about changing one's emotional and physical state to be something else. I experimented with it, and it could work well in the short term.

There was a side effect, though. It reinforced the notion that I couldn't trust anything coming from within me. That's because if I sensed an emotion in me, I had learned tools to change it to something else temporarily. (Tools I found destructive to use in the long term. So, I stopped using them. However, the damage was already done)

Later, in my late 20s, I reclaimed some of my power when I grew my beard and started living life on my terms.

But I now wanted to go much deeper and truly live from the heart.

How could I do that without being led astray or creating problems? What if I listened to something within me that led me down the wrong path? What if I wrongly mistake something stupid and random for inner wisdom? God knows I had screwed up a lot so far in life. I didn't want to create more problems for me.

So, I asked Camila, "How do I do that?"

She said, "Start by having someone ask you random questions about your preferences and desires. Then, listen to how your subconscious is responding. It might react loudly or very faintly. Immediately say out loud the first thing that comes up. Don't filter anything out. Don't think twice about it. Just say it out loud, no matter how crazy it sounds. "

Examples might be, "What ice cream do you prefer?" Or "What's your favorite thing to do when no one is watching?"

At the time, I was seeing a woman with whom I also had a good friendship. I told her what Camila said. As a result, she was enthusiastic about helping me. So we started having sessions where she'd ask many random personal questions. I'd then blurt out without any filters the first thing that came to mind.

Some answers were weird.
Some answers were sad.
Many answers were surprising.

It revealed a side of myself I was completely unfamiliar with. It existed beneath this mask I put on for society and myself. The mask of what I thought was acceptable.

Those questions also unveiled the deep loneliness and separation I felt from other people.

That started me into the habit of listening to what my subconscious was telling me about myself. But I had much more to learn.

Meditating

Later that year, I developed a friendship with Boniebelle, whom I met online. During our friendship, she told me she spent hundreds of hours developing her intuition through guided meditation. I was impressed by her dedication. I asked for her advice.

She sent me several guided meditation audios. One of those was the Past Life Regression by Doreen Virtue. The first half of the Past Life Regression takes the listener into a deep relaxation state. The second half then guides the listener through visual imagery of a couple of past lives. The idea is that by being guided into a past life, answers to the present problems can be found.

I didn't know if I had any past life. And whether I had any or not, I certainly couldn't say if anything that came up during such meditation was an actual past life. But I realized that didn't matter to me. What mattered to me was the wisdom. If it came 100% from my subconscious masquerading as a past life recollection, that would be ok, too.

I listened to my first one while lying in the bathtub. It was hard at first to lie down for this long, listening to a guided meditation. But I made it through, and I started listening to it once in a while.

Then, I met Boniebelle in person. I got to experience how incredibly intuitive she was in ways that blew my mind. She was able to figure things out intuitively about me and other people in a way that was light years ahead of anything else I had experienced.

Inspired by her examples, I dived deep into the past life regression-guided meditation. Getting into a deep relaxation state. Then, receive the wisdom from the guided imagery. Over the next few years, I listened to the meditation countless times. Honing in my ability to relax deeply. Then, listening inwardly. Getting valuable solutions, I couldn't have thought up logically.

Early on, I also struggled with my fears. How could I know if the signals I received internally were based on reactive fears or from a wiser source like my heart or intuition? While I was starting to face my fears, I still had so much anxiety about so many things in life. If I was to live aligned with love, instead of making fear-

219

based decisions, I needed to make heart-based decisions. I asked Boniebelle about this.

She advised me: "When you're looking at making a decision, take a moment to pause and reflect on the decision. Breathe deeply and then ask yourself, "What is the fear within me saying?". As it comes up, write down all the answers. Once you've written all that, breathe deeply and ask yourself, "What is the calm voice within me saying?". Then, pay attention to what is coming up and write that down. That will help you distinguish between what is a fear-based decision as opposed to what is a decision based on your inner guidance".

I started applying those two questions to almost every decision I made that involved an element of fear. It helped a lot in making sense of what was the voice of fear compared to the voice of wisdom, whether my heart, my intuition, or something beneficial within my subconscious, prodding me along.

After a year or two of doing the past life regression meditation, I started a new practice. I called it "GuMe" short for Guide Meditation. Each day, before starting my day, I'd sit still for 5-10 minutes. I'd breathe in deeply and quiet my mind. Then, I'd turn to what I considered my spiritual guides and see if I received any information regarding this day. It didn't matter whether the guidance came from my spiritual guides, my subconscious, or my heart. Before the busyness of the day, I wanted to touch in for a bit. Check to see if my inner voice was broadcasting anything I needed to pay attention to. Sometimes it didn't. Sometimes it did. I didn't do this every single day, but I aimed to.

David

Several years into my unemployment journey, looking to find my dream job, I entered the living room one evening while my mother watched TV. Sitting in the living room, I felt an urge to catch up and do the GuMe. I usually did GuMe in the morning, but I had skipped it that morning. So, I quieted my mind and pulled out my notepad. Then, I listened to what signals were coming from within me.

I received the message, "You need to go to this networking meeting tomorrow. There is someone you need to meet.".

I had attended several networking meetings a couple of years earlier. I found them to be a waste of time. I was also so awkward around them. So, I stopped going to them. I hadn't thought about them for a long time.

Receiving the guidance that I needed to go there to meet someone seemed a bit kooky to me. So, I ignored it.

The next morning, I followed my morning routine of going for a morning run. When I returned from my run, I sat down to do my usual GuMe. Cleared my mind. Listened to any guidance.

The same message came. "You need to go to that networking meeting. There is someone you need to meet".

How annoying, I thought. *Jeez. No way. I have way too many things to do. I'm not gonna waste 2-3 hours, feel awkward as hell, and then be behind on my task for that day.*

But I paused for a moment. What is the worst-case scenario? I'll waste 2-3 hours. What's the best-case scenario? I could make a fantastic connection. I had never received such inner guidance before. Maybe I could test it to see if it led to anything. I looked at the time and noticed I just had enough time to shower, get dressed, and make it to the meeting before it started.

I made it just in time. Walking into the meeting room, I wondered, "Who am I supposed to meet?". I mingled a little bit, feeling awkward as usual. Then I went to sit down in a chair. A presentation by a guest speaker was about to start.

The guest speaker turns out to be David Rawles from the nonprofit Career Solutions. It was the first time I had heard of him. However, as soon as he started his presentation, I was mesmerized. He talked with passion, deep knowledge, and heart about how to succeed in a job interview. His talk opened my eyes to much of what I was completely clueless about.

David then mentioned that through his nonprofit, he teaches a 12-week workshop series to prepare everything needed to land the job that people desire. It was free.

I then realized that this was the man I needed to meet. This was why I was guided to attend the networking meeting. I took down his information, the location, and the dates of his 12-week workshop.

Soon after, I started spending Thursday evenings at his workshop. I worked my way through the 12-week workshop. Then, I went through it a second time. It revolutionized my job search. I realized I had been doing so much, so completely ineffective. For example, instead of staying home and sending emails randomly, I needed to go out and network in person much more effectively—and do it in a way that isn't awkward. As a result, I completely changed my approach.

My inner voice had not let me down. It had been worthwhile to risk those 2-3 hours attending that meeting.

Dream Job Opening

Sometime later, I was doing a GuMe in the morning as usual. I now had a good resume and was regularly networking. I also conducted over a dozen information sessions with those working in my target industry. I periodically met and networked with other professionals looking for jobs. Instead of an amorphous "job I can do from the heart that is different from anything I have done before," I now had a specific target. It was a financial job in the nonprofit sector. My job search operation was vastly different than when I had initially met David.

However, on that early November morning, as I was doing a GuMe, I received a message from within.

I wrote in my journal:

> *"Look at your limiting beliefs about having a full-time job, and then work on overcoming them. Nothing else in November is as important as that."*
> *After the GuMe was over, I wrote in my journal:*
> *"Ok, what are all the deep reasons I don't want a job? What are the limiting beliefs about having a job?"*

As I journaled and listened to my subconscious, I realized that despite my deep desire to work full-time, a big part of me also resisted it. After five years of mainly being unemployed, I valued the freedom of how I spent my time.

During those years, I had spent significant time on my growth, shedding so much of my emotional and mental baggage. I also gained physical vibrancy and vitality. I learned that I could have an active social life by volunteering or attending free events despite having little to no income.

I had also reached the happiest I had ever been. I was experiencing a level far surpassing what I had previously experienced. I felt connected to myself, my emotions, my heart, my local community, and others on a level far exceeding what I had previously experienced. And did I mention I treasured my freedom to choose how I spent my time?

Yet, I still felt a deep desire to land a full-time job. I wanted to contribute something more significant to the world. I also wanted to be self-sufficient.

As I journaled, I saw that if I traded my time freedom, I needed to gain more than I was giving up. Financial compensation wouldn't be enough; instead, I needed the freedom to experience things at my job that I wouldn't be able to experience otherwise.

I reflected on that for the next few days. I finally wrote in my journal:

> *"Ok, what do I need to have in a job to make it worthwhile?"*
> *I wrote down:*
> *"1. I enjoy my work.*
> *2. I am trusted and respected.*
> *3. I work with coworkers that I like.*
> *4. I love my boss.*
> *5. I work for an organization whose mission helps the world in a way I resonate with."*

I put this list on my wall.

I then looked at other limiting beliefs I had regarding finding full-time employment. This was important. If a goal is like a destination I'm traveling by car to reach, I knew limiting beliefs would act as brakes. These limiting beliefs could stop me from achieving my goal if I didn't transmute them. So, I spent the rest of November examining and transmuting all the limiting beliefs I could find.

Job Opportunity

By the end of November, I attended my spiritual center's Sunday service after Thanksgiving. During that service, I heard an announcement from one of the ministers. She announced they had a full-time opening for a financial position within the center.

An unequivocal and thunderous voice within me rose and said internally, "That is your job."

After the service, I immediately went into action. I applied everything I had learned through David's workshop. First, I approached the minister, who announced the position. I asked her for a job description. She emailed it to me. When I read the description, I saw it was everything I had been looking for. Even though I had never had a job like it, I knew I had the skillset and education to do it well.

I also reflected. I loved the spiritual organization. I had volunteered in the organization's office a couple of years earlier. I loved how different and heart-centered it was compared to the corporate world I had worked in. Furthermore, the organization's leaders were powerful, heart-centered leaders who positively impacted people.

If I was going to give up a significant amount of my time freedom to work full-time, that was the job and the organization I'd be willing to do it for.

I sent a cover letter and resume following the format I learned in David's workshop. I was invited to an interview in early January.

I spent the next month preparing for the interview. On the day of the interview, I showed up fully prepared. A week later, I was given the job offer.

My inner voice had guided me well. It had prepared me well. Thankfully, I had listened to that inner voice to spend the month of November looking at my limiting beliefs. That was the last step in preparing me to land this dream full-time job. And now, instead of just learning to live from the heart, I would also learn to work from the heart. It had prepared me

Postscript

Six months later, as I was packing up to move my things into my apartment, I came across that list of the six things I required in my full-time work. It was what I would be willing to trade my time freedom to work full time. Reviewing that list, I realized I had every item in my current job.

My Reflection

Landing that full-time job didn't just mark the end of being mostly unemployed. It marked the conclusion of both an 8-year and a 15-year journey.

It was 15 years earlier when I had walked out of a career working in the aerospace industry. Instead of creating weapons of war, I wanted my job to be about contributing something positive to the world.

It was also almost eight years since I had gone on the green wig date with Josephine.

Now, I would get to join an organization devoted to living in alignment with love and helping people do so. This would start a new journey for me, one that helped me grow even more over the following years.

It had been a long journey for me to go from someone so disconnected from his heart, from other people, from his emotions, and from so many things to become so much more connected in all areas. It may have taken a long time for me, but I had to grow a lot to transform myself.

Learning to listen to that deep inner voice was critical in making it happen.

Your Reflection

How much do you trust the signals coming from within you?

How do you internally discern between a fear-based reaction and an intuitive heart-based response?

How much do you listen and follow that quiet inner voice within yourself?

(The inner voice might be a feeling, a picture, or a sensation and may not be an actual voice. It is often, but not always, quiet.)

Segue I

When it came time to create the cover for this book, I reached out to my friend Don. Don was an accomplished professional graphic artist who had created many book covers for other authors. I explained to Don my vision of having a photorealistic sun on the cover.

He asked, "What does the sun have to do with living from the heart?"

Initially, I couldn't verbalize an answer.

Later, I went outside and sat in the backyard under the sun. Then, I wrote down the answer to his question.

After I shared it with him, I decided to include the explanation in this book too.

Sun, Love, and Living from the Heart

Love is like the sun. It powers all that is good in our world.

Living from the heart is about accessing that power of love in all areas of life.

The sun powers Earth's life through photosynthesis, producing food for plant life. The sun also heats the planet, which makes the Earth warm enough for water to be present. Water, in turn, sustains almost all life on Earth.

When the sun is blocked through natural barriers (storms, trees, or rotation of the planet) or human-made obstacles (buildings, skyscrapers, walls), the sun's life-giving rays cannot reach the area below the barriers.

If plants are beneath the barrier, and if the barrier is up long enough, the plants will eventually die.

If an entire region is beneath the barrier (such as the Arctic during winter, which receives only a few hours of sun daily), it freezes. That leads to the inability of most life from being able to live there in the first place.

If humans are beneath the barrier, the lack of sun can seriously impede their ability to generate the vitamin D needed to function.

Love is like that, too. Love is ever-present in life, on Earth, and around us. When we form barriers that keep us from accessing that love, we cut ourselves off from that life-giving energy. Love doesn't go away. Instead, we can't access it and live from that place of love.

Barriers to accessing love include fears, disempowering beliefs, limiting habits, limiting self-identities, ignorance, and a lack of tools to overcome challenges and adversities.

The more we can remove these barriers and align ourselves with love, the more we can live from our hearts. The more we can live from our hearts, the more powerful we become, and the more good we can do in the world.

Then, just like the sun has a powerful and positive effect on the solar system and Earth, we can have a powerful and positive impact on those around us.

This book was about removing those barriers to love.

Segue II

A few drafts into the book, I realized I hadn't written my definition of what living from the heart would look like.

So, I wrote it up.

What it Means to Live
From The Heart

Living from the heart means recognizing that love flows through all of us. This means we align ourselves with the principle and energy of love as best as possible. We do this while realizing that, as humans, we may do this imperfectly. And that's ok.

Living from the heart means recognizing that our body is more than our mind and spirit. Our heart has a wisdom that must be heard to live our highest love-centered life.

Living from the heart means shedding those things that keep us from aligning with love. This can mean shedding limiting beliefs, habits, and fears. This can also mean shedding places, connections, and jobs that keep us from living from our hearts at the highest level.

Living from the heart means listening to and recognizing that our emotions are necessary signals from within. Whether they feel good or not, these signals let us know what is happening within us. Yet, it is also essential to recognize that emotions are just signals. They aren't the truth of a situation by themselves. They are the truth of what's happening within us, which may or may not align with reality.

Living from the heart requires us to face our fears head-on. Not just one time, but over and over. Living from the heart requires us to do things that may not be common, and that may not be popular. It also requires us to do things that may differ from what we are used to and what others want. Our heart doesn't care about what's popular, what our ego wants, or what other people's egos want. Our heart cares about the truth, love, and doing the right thing. That takes courage. Doing the courageous thing repeatedly helps us become more capable and able to face our fears. Thus, the more we exercise our courage, the greater our ability to live from the heart.

Living from the heart is about treating others with respect, dignity, and kindness. This isn't just about doing it on a superficial level but doing it profoundly. This is especially the case when we are triggered. Living from the heart means recognizing that what we dislike and hate in others usually reflects what we dislike and hate in ourselves. Or it's a reflection of a deep fear we have. Thus, living from the heart is about healing and making peace with that part of ourselves we dislike or hate. It's also about coming to terms with fear so that we can treat others with compassion, kindness, and dignity.

Living from the heart is about living within self-defined boundaries that keep us safe. We get to choose what those boundaries are. While we can and do treat others with love, we honor their boundaries as we honor our own. Living from the heart does not mean we become beings to be trampled upon. Instead, we ensure our boundaries are honored. All the while spreading love into the world.

Living from the heart means ensuring we care for ourselves and thus build a solid foundation to help others. It means cleaning up what isn't working in our lives. It means ensuring our physical, spiritual, emotional, and mental needs are met at the deepest level possible. With this foundation in place, we are better able to help others.

Living from the heart is about recognizing that our world isn't perfect and that there are things we want to change. Rather than sitting back and pointing fingers at others, living from the heart means we become the change we wish to see in the world.

Living from the heart means actively aiming to do good in the world. We actively seek to improve other people's lives. Or we help improve organizations. Or we take care of what needs to be done. This might mean improving our skill sets to better contribute to the world what may be uniquely ours to contribute. It might mean being kind and extra supportive to other people around us. It might mean doing what is in front of us, whatever that might be, in the best way we can for the good of others. Regardless, we are a beneficial presence on this planet, and we aim to continue improving how we show up.

Living from the heart at the highest level means we become aware of who we are at the deepest level. We become aware of our values, dreams, and who we are at our highest self. By knowing and understanding ourselves on a deep level, we also get to know others on a deep level. By knowing others deeply, we love and accept them as they are.

Living from our heart means we forgive ourselves for falling short of our ideals. It also means we forgive others when they fall short of our ideals or theirs. Forgiveness does not come with complacency. It comes with a willingness to try again, learn from our failures, and improve at living from the heart.

Living from the heart is a unique journey for each of us. While there are bases upon which to build, how we progress, and approach things will look different. Living from the heart may look different for each of us.

Learning to live from the heart is a never-ending process. It isn't a one-and-done type of thing. It isn't an accomplishment that we can check and say, "OK, done." It's an ideal, one that is constantly refined and aimed for. We may be imperfect at this. We may screw up. That is ok and is part of the journey. The important thing is to recognize when that happens. With that recognition, we can learn our lesson and return to living from the heart. What matters is that this year, we are living from the heart more than we were last year. And that next year, we will be better at living from the heart than we were this year. Perfection isn't the goal. Progress is.

Afterword

"Yesterday, I was so clever, so I wanted to change the world. Today I am wise, so I am changing myself." - Rumi

Writing this book changed me.

After writing a few drafts of this book, in December of 2021, I went to a retreat at a Llama Farm in Northern Georgia. It was just me, my iPad, my wireless keyboard, and some llamas on the farm. Besides my close friend Michael Dewey, nobody else had yet to read any chapters from my book. Michael, who had volunteered to serve as my editor, had read the first few chapters. However, he died in April 2021. I felt a bit lost.

During the retreat, I went within and asked for guidance on what I needed to do to move things forward with the book. The answer I received within me was, "Let go of your identity of being an intensely private person. Adopt the identity of being a public person instead.". That didn't mean privately sharing everything about my life. I'd still have privacy. But it meant sharing a whole lot more about my life. It meant no longer hiding in public. It meant sharing what mattered to me with the world at large.

I felt a mix of fear and humbleness upon receiving this inner guidance. Carrying out this change would be such a massive shift for me. However, I saw how adopting the new identity would help me get ready to publish my memoir. It would also help me get ready to make an impact beyond the book. After soaking these realizations, I went to the edge of the pond. I stood up, faced the sky with my arms stretched out. I then tenderly asked the universe to support me. I'd need all the help I could get to make this inner change.

For the following year, I mostly paused the work on my book. Instead, I wrote and publicly shared many stories and thoughts on Facebook. These were stories and thoughts I once guarded very closely to my chest. Most of the time, I felt such fear and trepidation before making my post. That would be followed by relief and joy at seeing my friends and acquaintances' responses. That year, I went by the mantra, "If I'm afraid of sharing it, I must share it."

I slowly started seeing how what I shared on social media entered my real life. I'd have people who read my posts tell me on the phone or in person how my stories inspired them or how much they loved it. It helped me see myself as more of a public person who is more willing to share some of his stories. It also helped me find more of my voice. By the end of that year, I was ready to resume working on the book.

I also had to face one of my greatest demons: The demon of "Not enough time." I was working full-time in challenging roles that impacted the organizations I worked for. How could I spend time working on a book with all the pressure I faced? I slowly learned to face that demon and eventually carved out time most days to work on this book for many months at a time.

Working on this book also helped me make peace with so much of my past. For example, before writing this book, I was somewhat ashamed of having spent five and a half years in my 30s mostly unemployed. I used to carefully keep that part of my life hidden. However, writing these stories helped me see how those years helped me grow tremendously. What I did during that time helped set me up for the success I encountered afterward. Not just the outward success but also the success in becoming more of the kind of man and human being I wanted to become. As a result, I'm now proud of that period of my life.

The hardest chapter for me to share was "Living Life on My Terms: The Tale of the Bearded Man's Way of Life". Before writing the book, I had never told that story to anyone except succinctly to one close friend. That friend had shared with me an incident they had with suicide ideation. It was so deeply ingrained within me that this was the most taboo topic of all.

To get ready to include this story in my book, I borrowed from the strategies I shared in the chapter "Releasing Shame: The Tale of the Interview." First, I told the story to my counselor and then to my best friend. Then, I started sharing it with some of my other friends one by one. Sometimes by phone. Sometimes in person. Always from a tender place. Then, one evening, I shared the story with the group of men in my circle of men. After that, I was finally ready to include the story in this book.

Next, writing this book has been a significant exercise in trust. When I began writing this book, I had no idea how to write a book. There was so much unknown. It was overwhelming. So, I instead simply focused on doing the next step. I'd continuously trust that once that step was over, I'd be guided to the next step. I also dived deeper into trusting that the universe had my back during this whole process.

When it came time to decide whether to publish this book or not, I reflected on the journey I had been on. I felt that even if I never published my memoir, writing It was worth it as it helped me grow significantly.

Stephan
July 10, 2024

Acknowledgments

I am grateful to many people for encouraging me as I wrote this book.

I also want to express my gratitude to these individuals:

Michael Dewey (1961-2021) for volunteering to serve as my editor. Michael was the first to read the first few chapters. His encouragement and advice were crucial in helping me get started.

Stephanie Roman (1984-2021) encouraged me early on so much to write this book. I know she is on the other side, cheering me on.

My mother, Marline Collins, was almost always the first to read each chapter's draft (besides the first few Michael had first read), providing valuable feedback and encouragement.

Don Huff for creating the beautiful book cover.

Jim Elsener for proofreading an earlier draft.

Kim Butler, Don Huff, Melissa Votja, and Wesley Hart for reading earlier drafts of the book and providing valuable feedback and suggestions.

Emilee Evans, my accountability and productivity coach from Commit Action, for being a vital force in making sure I not only moved forward with the book but finished it.

Emails

Il'd love your feedback, whether it be about which chapter you liked the most, what you got out of the book, what didn't resonate with you, or anything else (including spelling/grammar corrections!) Email me at stephanfeedback@gmail.com.